BRUISED YET PRICELESS

UNDERSTANDING YOUR VALUE THROUGH

GOD'S APPRAISAL PROCESS

BY

SEAN CORT

Bruised Yet Priceless

Copyright ©2011 by Sean Cort

Bruised Yet Priceless

Understanding Your Value Through God's Appraisal Process

Printed in the United States of America

ISBN 978-0-9832399-0-1

All rights reserved solely by the author. The author guarantees all contents are original and do not infringe upon the legal rights of any other person or work. No part of this book may be reproduced in any form without the permission of the author. The views expressed in this book are not necessarily those of the publisher.

Unless otherwise indicated, Bible quotations are taken from the HOLY BIBLE, NEW INTERNATIONAL VERSION®.
Copyright © 1973, 1978, 1984 by International Bible Society. Used by permission of Zondervan Publishing House.

www.trueperspectivepublishinghouse.com

ACKNOWLEDGEMENTS

For my Lord and Savior Jesus Christ, I devote all I am and all I do to your glory for acceptance as my offering of thanksgiving and worship. Lord, in You alone do I live and breathe.

For the countless women and faceless others whom we have known to pass from this life without the empowerment of knowing their value and their legacy.

Every person who goes through a wilderness experience or the spiritual warfare that comes with the Christian walk will get a little beat up and even abused. We all at some time need to be picked up and dusted off so that we can be reminded of the love that restores. Because of Calvary, none of us were placed here for abuse.

For every living girl and woman who stands at the doorway to destiny with their back to a hurtful past, I challenge you to lift your head and look through this doorway toward the hills from which cometh your help. Pick up the legacy from some of those who have crawled, stumbled and limped with dignity. Embrace the legacy for others who stood straight despite their broken pride and graciously press through that doorway toward the mark of the high calling in Christ Jesus.

I am here to tell you that Jesus deemed you PRICELESS before and during your most difficult times. This is why you are still here to help someone else to their feet that are standing behind you.

For my spiritual father, Bishop Joseph Nathaniel Williams, thank you for your spiritual covering and for reminding me of my value.

AUTOGRAPH PAGE

Because of your value; autograph this book to
yourself or
someone else you value.

CONTENTS

INTRODUCTION..................................xi

<u>**Chapter One**</u>

BETRAYAL

Never Alone 1

Everyday Betrayal 3

First Betrayal……………………………......6

Creaking Boards………………………….10

The Grass Isn't Even Real…………….…...13

Pain Has a Sound……………….…..……...19

When the Church Betrays You……………....21

Hidden in Plain Sight………………….…...25

Can Anyone Hear Me……………….……...31

Finding Purpose for Your Betrayal…………..34

Chapter Two

THE BRUISING PROCESS

Find a Corner..45

Damage Assessment...................................48

Your Secret Place...51

Your Condition Will Not Be Your Outcome....55

Chapter Three

TAKING DOMINION

The Thought Process....................................63

Awareness...68

Rules of Engagement...................................71

Holy Spirit Morning Greeting.......................75

Accept the Facts...76

Declarations..81

No More Fear...84

Declarations of Intent...................................87

Taking Dominion……………………..………90

Chapter Four

THE FORGIVING PROCESS

Pennies for Your Thoughts…………….…...93

I'm Stuck…………………………...…………..96

Just the Facts ………………...……………....99

Let He Who is Without Sin………………..105

Obedience……………………………………..111

The Hardest Thing to Do…………………..116

Scriptures on Forgiveness…………………121

Chapter Five

ME TIME

What is Me Time………………………….....133

Rehearsal Has Been Cancelled…………….135

Some Assembly Required…………………..136

Who Am I ?...141

Here is How...144

Knowledge is Power............................146

Be the Thermostat Not the Thermometer.....147

The Total Package...............................149

Chapter Six

PRICELESS

Exceedingly and Abundantly.,..................151

The Christmas Challenge......................163

Play Well With Others.........................167

This is for Calvary..............................169

All That Matters................................173

What Now?......................................176

INTRODUCTION

We all have a story to tell as you have seen on the many reality TV shows and varied social networking sites on the web. But before these avenues of transference existed between people, we all had to find our way somehow to get our point across. With some it was their fashion sense while with others it was their manner of speech and behavior. Even still--the fact is, what is the true story about us? Who can we be authentic with and most of all; can we be authentic with ourselves?

It's obvious by the cover that this book is primarily targeted to the woman who has a story, but like her social security number and I.D. is very private and never shared unless absolutely necessary. Furthermore the people you share this information with are in a profession that knows the cover of your book but will never get to read the story within its pages.

Bruised Yet Priceless is that companion that will revisit the origin of each of those stories and walk you through their intent and their value. After getting better acquainted with you and earning your trust; with your permission, this book will help you at the most personal and spiritual level to deal with those issues as though sitting on the lap of the guardian you wish you always had.

This guardian will not judge nor will they be harsh. This guardian will merely help you to do what only you can decide to do; have the funeral for the old and celebrate the birth of the new. This book will teach you how to transition from the victim to the victor, the thermometer to the thermostat and the you that God intended on you being when He created you.

It's not too late; it's never too late. It's not too hard because the transition will be your personal revolution from within. Every revolution comes about as a result of desperation and/or timing. You are about to encounter a revolution from within. You were never created to fail. Your failed battles and seasons are mere assignments filled with tasks that you must check off and complete successfully in order to move on

At the conclusion of this book you will never again live beneath your privilege nor will anyone else you love and touch, because you will understand and embrace your priceless value and purpose in this life.

Bruised Yet Priceless

CHAPTER ONE
BETRAYAL

You are reading this book because you have an expectation of something. I trust that expectation is truth. I promise you have truth in your hands right now. Regardless of what you have endured, just know that if you pursue truth, it will never deceive you nor will it sneak up and surprise you.

No one will ever have -its newer version. Even if –it's new to you, it will instinctively bond to and complete what you already know. When truth shows up, never question it and never abuse it. Truth doesn't need you; - you need it. Truth merits no reward, nor does it dignify a response. Truth is absolute-and therefore supreme.

NEVER ALONE

When a feeling of betrayal comes along, it has the uncanny ability to make us feel as though we are the only one encountering its cold and sinister intentions. This enemy has a way of making us feel twisted and dysfunctional as a result of what was done to us. I am here to tell you, that is a lie from the master of all lies. He operates through isolation and fear.

If he can isolate you and strip you down of all you had of value, then he can frighten you into remaining in your nightgown and slippers. You will be too scared to venture out from your safety zone to see the true life God has prepared for you. Like an oppressive marriage, the enemy can hold you captive to your fears of the unknown. As a result, you can condemn yourself to spiritual and emotional bankruptcy. The truths assembled for you in this book will build upon each other from chapter to chapter.

Don't skip through them as so many skip through the lives and faces they encounter every day. Take the time to analyze the treasure in each story. Make it a point to store that story in your experiential repertoire for the person God sends your way who may be in need of some "out of the box" wisdom that they wouldn't expect to hear from someone packaged liked you. They will then experience the adage, "never judge a book by its cover."

> *The fact is, as a result of Adam and Eve's sin, we all must go through some place ugly in order to arrive at some place beautiful.*

Your painful experiences are part of God's appraisal value for you. The extent of the discomfort endured will bring your appraisal value up from for the place you've come to. We are all in this place together and we owe it to our God, Jehovah Nissi, the Hebrew translation for *our God of love and protection,* to tell how such evil could be transformed into such good. My friend, this chapter is a small sampling of the varied and extreme circumstances and day to day issues some of us have gone through. Oh no! You are not alone.

EVERYDAY BETRAYAL

One morning I was driving down a main road in the town we live. It was about 8:45 and I was on my way to my usual 9 a.m. Friday barber's appointment. I took careful note of the time because I was actually on time this morning. Although I try to squeeze the last second out of every minute of every day, it didn't bother me when I encountered a stop light that was unusually long. Traffic had already been a bit slow because this particular road was in the midst of a major widening project.

If there were two more of me and about another 12 hours in a day, I would be so elated at the fact that my days would actually be filled with absolute completion. I'm always multi-tasking spiritually and mentally, which always seems to leave me with just enough time. So as I sat at this unusually long light I had some extra time to visually explore the construction site. Construction sites, especially road projects, have been a fascination of mine since I was a child. That essentially means the past is truly the present. I consider myself still to be a fun-loving, transparent child at heart.

I've always been fascinated with the correct process and methodology with how things are done. Even if it makes no sense to me why things take so long, they do so for a specific reason. As I had these thoughts, I noticed the reason for the delay was the crew was moving a huge piece of equipment across the highway to the other side so the crew on the other side of the highway could replicate what the other crew was doing. The signal guys were manually operating the traffic light to safely accommodate their duties.

Just then I realized a cricket-like sound almost directly above my head. It turned out to be a power line. Power lines are something that is common in every-day life, depending on where in the world you live. Big cities house their power lines below ground and rural and suburban areas have them mounted on posts.

This was the first time that I imagined being this close to one for this period of time. I followed the buzzing sound to one of the poles and pinpointed where the sound was coming from. Amazing, I thought to myself. There was a sign about the size of my license plate that read, "Danger, High Voltage."

So here I was, sitting in traffic and about 30 feet above my head was a power line with at least 35,000 volts of electricity. So I thought to myself, "If I was mischievous and curious enough, I could cause myself and others some serious damage."
Then I thought again, "Why is something so dangerous, so close to the roadway?"

So here's my point. There are so many aspects of our every-day life that bring us so much potential danger that we are not even aware of it. These dangers are sometimes as obvious as the nose on your face, like those power lines. Some dangers are not as obvious, yet they can easily be detected if you're in the right frame of mind to observe and understand them.

Take for instance the strange rule of having to wear seatbelts in an airliner while it's taxiing on solid tarmac at 20 miles per hour (mph), but at 30,000 feet and traveling at 450 mph, it's considered safe to remove the seatbelt.

The inherent danger here is if the plane suddenly hits a wind shear your head would immediately hit the ceiling at 200 mph. To me, all of these instances are considered betrayals. Nothing is as it appears. Here's an example; consider all the ice that fast food restaurants place in your beverage cup. How much ice does that soda or water need? When you look at it you are only getting half a cup of beverage. There seems to be no safe haven anymore.

Medicine has tricked us into believing that treatment is better than the cure. Our national leaders are well aware of threats against our national security, lives and welfare, but keep us in the dark to avoid mass panic. Doctors, teachers, law enforcement personnel, care givers, lawyers and politicians sign on to do a job that is steeped in the integrity of being given authority and fiduciary responsibility to protect, yet many pervert this authority for personal gain.

All of us in one way or another have been misled, misrepresented or ill-treated. Depending on your personality type, at least one of your first responses will be with a feeling of betrayal.

FIRST BETRAYAL

We all can think back to the point in our lives where we remember being lied to or lied on for the first time. To think someone actually took something from you that you couldn't place in a box: your trust. Maybe you were too young to really weigh the gravity of this first betrayal but it didn't feel right.

Maybe your first feelings of betrayal occurred when you opened up that gift and the batteries were put in and you switched it on and nothing happened. It didn't do what it was supposed to do. *How could that be? It's new, it was bought for me and no one had it before. So how could it be broken already?*

How about the early childhood skirmishes at school where either something was broken or mysteriously vanished or you received all the screen credit in this dramatic series of events? Here you are totally innocent of wrongdoing and you are faced with the penalty.

You learned for the first time what it felt like to be lied on and falsely accused. Whether this was deliberately planned to get you in trouble by some sinister fellow classmate or it was purely a case of mistaken implication. As time would reveal, life will later afford you the opportunity to get away with things that you are never implicated in; bittersweet is the phrase you will understand.

Let's not forget the quintessential example of someone betraying your trust. You know the story. You tell someone a secret, your first secret. A secret that today would make you smile and even giggle about its simplicity. But at that time you didn't want God to know about it. Any disloyalty from a confidant would seem like an act of treason in a time of war punishable by death-your death.

When you least suspected it the very secret and personal thing that you shared with a soul outside of your own is heard by you coming from another person's lips. This time there is ridicule and perhaps scorn attached to this precious story that you once entrusted to a friend.

This secret may have been about your first crush, your first lie that you cared to share or even worse; something deeply personal that you did or realized about yourself. Now you are left injured by the roadside as the quickly approaching bus pulled you under and threw you to the side of the road, naked and bruised for all to laugh and stare at.

You eventually get over the fact that you hate everybody within 100 feet and the fact that everyone in the free world now knows your secret. How painful and embarrassing, yet every educational. When we look back over these childhood memories, their innocence almost brings a smile and even a soft giggle to your spirit. These thoughts somehow bring about a comforting blanket of normalcy as if that would have been the only forms of betrayal we would have ever had.

First betrayal isn't always as academic or benign. First betrayals for some of us strike us to the core of our existence with bone -chilling accuracy with almost immediate paralysis. For those of us who share this feeling, there isn't any warm smile and certainly no comfort of any kind, unless shards of glass getting caught in y our eyelids bring comfort to you. Too harsh a choice of words? At least we have the advantage of easily discounting experiences in this manner.

Right now as we speak, there is a child somewhere experiencing horrors that would make the most hardened death row inmate grimace and turn their head away if video cameras were present in that child's world right now. As resilient as the nature and the Spirit of God in these children would have it, they get up the next day end continue to exist. Some of you were once those children who have grown up and are reading these pages now.

Some of these betrayals have come by the hand of family members and even parents. These are the people who violate a trust that even some species of wild animals would never contemplate. Some have gone onto to become adults who have vowed to never parent a child because of the fear that the same demons secretly lurk within them too.

Some of these bruised children have grown to become parents who vow a lifetime of love and devotion to their children as an act of faith to finally kill and cremate the remains of these evil beings that return within to remind them of who they once were.

Some of the memories that may haunt your spirit may include rape, incest, sodomy, physical abuse, verbal abuse, mental abuse, isolation, fear tactics, starvation, exploitation, enslavement, abduction, hypnotism, witchcraft, manipulation, exposure to pornography, and countless other horrific actions. Being placed in these situations leave most feeling as though if there is a God then He must not care about me. So if He does not care about me then I don't care about Him either.

I have spent over 20 years in ministry, talk show production and consulting with companies in a wide array of industries. During these experiences you get to meet, interview and counsel lots of people while listening to their stories. In fact, just in living and experiencing life's people you may have heard or read about some of the same stories.

CREAKING BOARDS

Let's take for instance a young lady we'll call Dawn. Her father and she were extremely close. Growing up in the rural south of the U.S. in the early 1970's there was lots of free time when the sun went down. When her ailing mother was asleep her dad would put a teaspoon of brandy in her little brother's night time glass of milk to get him asleep.

When he finally fell asleep she and her dad would stay up on the porch and count fire flies and see who could count the most in an hour. They enjoyed sweet innocent time together playing checkers and making up scary stories about what really lurked in the corn fields after the clock struck midnight.

One night when Dawn found it real challenging to fall asleep she sat on the edge of her bed to see if her toes could easily touch the floor from her bed. She would do this once a week to measure how much she was growing as a result from all the milk she was drinking every night. Her daddy always told her that if she drank milk every day that she would grow to be taller and stronger than her daddy.

This particular night the creaking boards that she would hear coming from down the hallway seemed louder than usual. She used to complain to her dad, saying that sometimes the creaking boards would wake her up at night. Her dad would always tell her it's the house settling.

This particular night since she was wide awake she could tell that this time the creaking was actual footsteps. She got up and snuck over to her door and slowly opened it. She saw her brother's door slightly opened and tiptoed to his room to see what was going on.

She opened the door slowly and couldn't believe what she saw. The horror was worse than any story she and her dad would attempt to outdo each other with on the front porch. Dawn saw her dad, her hero and best friend, removing her brother's underwear and fondling him while he was asleep. She was frozen and numb. She watched as he started to do the unthinkable and screamed, "Daddy, don't!" Her voice even startled her as her own shrill was unlike any she had ever heard in her life.

Her brother was too knocked out to even know what was happening but Dawn was wide awake and she was never the same again. Up until now she had never suffered disappointment in any form. She and her brother had never even received a spanking or been on the wrong end of harsh words from either parent.

Into each life some rain must fall. Dawn's life up to this point was pretty much a storybook fantasy. That night marked Dawn's arrival to womanhood because she had to assume the role of a mother and night watch commander over her brother's innocent body.

Needless to say, Dawn and her father were never the same again. Her mother eventually died from her illness and she was left to raise her brother while watching her father. She never spoke to her dad about his actions on that night and certainly never told her brother. Her dad's actions were a harsh betrayal and she never forgave him, even though he tried to pretend that she was still his buddy.

Dawn was civil to keep the peace but to this day is n ot on good terms with him. Now as a woman Dawn is able is understand her father's loneliness as a result of her mother's constant illness. What she couldn't understand was how a father could use his innocent child to satisfy his manly urges. All she could rehearse in her head was how the possibility that this heinous act may have occurred on several occasions due to the countless nights of the floor boards creaking.

Dawn eventually got m arried and moved away after she saw that her brother was enjoying college life away from home. The dad's behavior changed toward the brother immediately from that night, so they were never close as he grew up. Here is a case where the sexually molested victim was able to have his mental innocence preserved although the guardian is the one who suffered the scarring.

THE GRASS ISN'T EVEN REAL

Nothing screams betrayal more to most than when your partner, confidant and spouse cheats on you and commits sexual and emotional infidelity. In hindsight most who have been on the receiving side of this experience find it difficult to decipher which causes more pain; the sexual infidelity or the emotional infidelity. Some women have told me that the emotional infidelity was what ultimately caused the demise of the relationship, even after they took him back for cheating sexually.

These women told me that it would actually hurt less if it were a one-night stand with a prostitute than the co-worker he saw and had lunch with every day. The men I've spoken to had mixed feelings. Most had more of a problem with the sexual infidelity than the emotional aspect.

Counseling in a ministerial capacity, most of the men had a problem with giving up the physical territory of the relationship before the emotional or intellectual portions.

As quiet as it's kept, women are just as territorial as men are concerning their relationships. Men tend to be more territorial over the physical rights of their relationships with their women than the emotional or intellectual.

Please understand that not all men feel this way, but a great many of us do. The biggest part of a man's need in any relationship is the respect of his woman. Most women have a connection with their girlfriends or gay male friends that don't threaten most men.

This bond is based on simple commonalities and more significant intellectual connections. Some men feel at ease with this since it means that there is balance and one less thing on his "honey-do list." But as soon as there is a ny attraction or touch, all bets are off.

This is where the same hunter/gatherer instinct that pursued the woman comes into play. Women on the other hand tend to be more territorial about the whole package of their man. The women I have counseled in ministry and interviewed while hosting talk shows - don't want to share any part of their man, other than watching the game with Joe or Bob on an occasional weekend. Even in those cases, she wants to know that Joe or Bob do not pose a threat to her and her man's stability.

In other words, Joe and Bob better be in a committed and stable relationship. If Joe or Bob have any "player" intentions, she does not want them infecting her husband and posing a threat to what she worked hard to build and maintain. So suffice it to say that women don't want their man coming into contact with any resemblance of emotional infidelity with a heterosexual woman-- or man for that matter.

Some women I've encountered gage emotional infidelity as grounds alone for a breakup. In their eyes once you've shared a piece of your heart with someone else then with time the body is just a matter of convenience.

This sets the stage for my introduction of a couple we'll call Mike and Toni. They are a fun-loving couple that has been married for only three years. They dated for two years before they got engaged. During their 16-month engagement they received pre-marital counseling from their pastor. So in total they have been together for five-plus years. Are you with me so far?

Mike pursued Toni the moment he saw her as keenly as a bloodhound on a scent. She was striking and carried herself with a confidence that caught his attention. Toni admired his tenacity and polish until she finally caved to his persistence. She loved the way he treated people and loved even more, the way he made her feel as though she was the only person in the room. Fast forward six and a half years later; they have just celebrated their third wedding anniversary.

Things are really taking off for Toni in her high powered corporate role and she is now traveling more than she ever anticipated. When she and Mike got married it was Mike whose career was booming and Toni who was still finishing up her degree. Toni used to always tell Mike that she would always be there to make his favorite dinner (baked ziti) fresh from the oven on a weekly basis.

The couple had a very physical relationship, so Mike had grown use to their sexual intimacy at least every other night. Toni had to travel at least four nights out of the week and the nights varied from week to week.

Mike knew that one day they would have children and that he would have to share Toni with someone else, but he never figured it would come so soon and so rudely into his life.

You've heard the story before, I'm sure. Eventually Mike's support of his corporate super star wife began to fade and soon turned to resentment. His sarcastic stabs replaced the words he once used to soothe her after a long day and motivate her the next morning. Toni tried to be understanding, but she too got tired of the jeers and sexist remarks that she already received from her male co-workers.

Mike became increasingly resentful and started confiding in his female co-workers about his matrimonial issues. Eventually one of the female friends extended more sympathy than the others as they both now planned to work late together so they would be able to be alone.

As Mike was beginning his walk down the slippery slope of emotional infidelity, Toni found the shoulder of her mentor at work to cry on. The shoulder became an embrace. Eventually, they started planning business trips to the same city so that they too, would have the opportunity to be alone.

As time went on both Mike and Toni both knew the lifestyle they pursued was not right before God or within the promises of their covenant with God. As if the closing bell rang on the floor of the New York Stock Exchange, both of them decided to end their extra-marital pursuits—on almost the same day.

Neither of them admitted to me what actually took place, but I made it clear that they needed to at least come clean with each other and the Lord. In our last counseling session, Toni broke down and pleaded with Mike to forgive her for not being there for him. She felt as though she had turned him out on the street to fend for himself. She got so caught up in making the money that she forgot that he was her treasure.

Mike admitted to being emotionally unfaithful and that he broke his biggest promise to her and that was never to place his hurt or fears in anyone else but her and the Lord. He told her he didn't even care if she was physically unfaithful to him because he stopped protecting her the moment he started attacking her. So therefore he was grateful that someone else was there to protect her from him.

PAIN HAS A SOUND

Although not typical of most marriages that suffer divorce, Mike and Toni could have easily have gone there. Most couples who are put in this situation try to explore greener pastures just to see that there is a better place else where or that there is a cliff just after 10 feet of grass. But they decided their love is stronger than the pain.

It may not have been as romantic or as sweet for you. Perhaps there were some other nuances in your break- up that made your choice to go irrevocable. For some women it may have been a steel pipe that her husband got hold of during that last argument in the garage.

Maybe it was the things he brought up about the deepest darkest part of your life that you made him vow to never breathe a word about. Then you realize his hatred for you that moment was so deep that he never hesitated thrusting that dagger into your beating heart. You think to yourself, "What if the gun was nearby? Would he have gone for that instead?"

Either way you feel just as numb and lifeless. Everything seems to have gone painfully silent and now you are watching your life unfold through a television monitor from another room. You see his face and you hear his muffled words but it doesn't even matter anymore. All you hear is your pulse and your chest filling up and squeezing out air.

You're not sure if you slapped him, threw something at him or if you called him something you never thought you would say to a living soul. It doesn't matter. You have already decided in your core of existence that it will never be the same again. In fact, as long as you're concerned, it's over.

Too much violence for you? How about the simple fact that the one-night stand that he claimed he never had gave you the sexually-transmitted disease that just keeps giving and giving? Now you're alone and have this issue that will label you as damaged goods for the rest of your life.

You smile every time you meet someone new, but the label keeps reminding you that the other side is sticky and that it's not going anywhere. So beautiful is the rose but a there is a slight bruise on the petal. Does anyone buy imperfect single long-stemmed roses anymore? Are you still a rose that someone can still cherish despite the bruise? Or will God have mercy on you and miraculously air brush the blemish from your picture forever? That's my hope too.

Not all betrayals in relationships have to do

with people. Some of us stay in committed relationships for 20 and 30 years to jobs and companies. We serve these institutions faithfully and have even sacrificed our health and happiness for the sake of loyalty and one day getting that gold watch and a great retirement.

One day you return from a much needed vacation and are told with no emotion or sympathy, that you are no longer needed or wanted; pack your things.

It's like being hit with a pillow and having the lights turned out. "Surely this is a joke—right?" You think to yourself. No it's not. Now what? After all these years you've tied your identity with the role you have served at this company. Now where is your identity? It's bad enough you were never compensated consistently with your performance or experience, but now to add insult to injury, they just let you go, just like that. Life is so cold and people can be so cruel.

WHEN THE CHURCH BETRAYS YOU

The church is supposed to be a safe haven from those who mean us ill-will. When we were children some of us had parents who told us that there were certain people and places that were safe for us to talk to and go to in the event of an emergency. If the church was in your neighborhood then this was likely one of those places.

As we grew up we've learned a certain degree of respect for the church and its leadership. Do you remember playing tag with your friends as a child? You'll remember that there was always a base and that was the safe place. In life, church is supposed to be a safe place.

> *As I've grown in my faith I've learned there is a distinct difference between worshipping the man of God and worshipping the God of man. The former will bring you pain and disappointment while the latter will heal and restore you.*

There is nothing more important in this life than understanding which master you serve. John 10:27-30 affirms this by saying, *"My sheep listen to my voice; I know them, and they follow me. I give them eternal life, and they shall never perish; no one can snatch them out of my hand. My Father, who has given them to me, is greater than all; no one can snatch them out of my Father's hand. I and the Father are one."*

> *Fewer things in life hurt more than when your betrayal comes from within your own support system.*

The church has always been the safe refuge for all who seek it, despite what we look like, what we've done and who we are. This is where we bring our broken spirit, our marriage that hangs in the balance, our wayward children and every other troubling situation or decision that needs to be healed.

The hand that stands at the door to receive us in these fragile conditions are hands that are nurturing and clean. No one is perfect but we expect the church worker and the leader to at least be in a stronger position spiritually than we are.

That's where the ideals stop and reality should begin. The fact is in today's society most of what appears one way is completely the opposite. We have always expected a fair degree of corruption in politics and big business in our country--and most other places. But we tend to be a bit more careful when applying these labels to the church worker in the house of God.

Remember what I said about worshipping the God of man and not the man of God? I hope so 'because what I'm about to share may make you run for the hills.

As mentioned, I've been blessed with a rich professional life in corporate America. At the writing of these words on my ecumenical resume I have been an ordained elder for over 16 years and I have been actively serving in various ministerial capacities for over 23 years. I have been an assistant pastor, evangelist, altar worker, prayer line operator/intercessory prayer warrior, Christian radio/TV, music and talk show host and producer, ministerial counselor and mentor to young children and adults of all ages.

I've had the privilege to consult numerous inner-city grassroots organizations and churches. I also have the honor of consulting the marketing and community campaigns for some notable churches in the U.S. I have also ghostwritten and created Bible class lesson for these same mega ministries.

This is not to self-promote but to establish the platform from which I draw the wealth of experience I share in this book for the overall betterment of the Kingdom of God. The facts that I am to share are not done as an indictment to any one man or woman in the church. This information is to serve as a road sign of what you may encounter if you are too naïve and your spirit is not attuned to God. In the same way someone would warn you about black ice on the road or the risk of speed traps, this information should serve as a warning.

Truth is sometimes confrontational to those who don't like the way it's packaged.

> ***Truth warrants no reward nor does it dignify a response. Truth, like God is sovereign, and therefore requires no explanation.***

You will hear this several times throughout this book.

HIDDEN IN PLAIN SIGHT

This is the best way to cloak the most sinister modality of attack upon an unsuspecting enemy. We as human beings become such creatures of habit that take things for granted so easily that we seldom notice subtle signs of trouble. Think of the news stories we've heard about horrible acts of murder and suicide. Most eyewitnesses say that they never suspected a thing.

Most clinically-depressed people or those suffering from deep mental health issues can become better actors than the Hollywood "A List." These folks, some of us included, have a critical desire to be helped but an even more desperate desire to fit in and be accepted.

They know that if they are found out that they will become labeled and despised by society and their once supportive network of friends and loved ones. To take this a step deeper over in the spiritual realm, the spiritual manifestations that drive mankind to do evil things prefer to remain hidden.

This is why children can be exposed to something heinous at the age of four and show no outward manifestation or damage until much later in life. *These spiritual manifestations, like a creature of prey can lay in wait much longer than we can pay attention.*

For more information on this topic read chapter eight, "Breaking Generational Curses" in my book, *The Power of Perspective*. The same way these manifestations can remain hidden in us and our next-door neighbor is the same way they can be hidden in our clergy and other church workers. This is not like living in the Old Testament of the Bible where if a man of God or a priest commits sin that he must immediately make an offering to God or be struck dead. Today we live under the dispensation of grace.

This dispensation adds room or a grace period in order to get it right and get it right with the love of the Lord. Jesus didn't come to break Levitical law; He came to fulfill the law. Most Christians only know of the Ten Commandments that Moses brought down from the mountain.

There were actually 613 laws listed in the Torah, which is the core of the Hebrew Bible. God was and will always be a God of love, but His love was not reflected in the way that the Levites administered His laws. Jesus came to fulfill God's love for His people by giving them the grace through acceptance of His Son to get it right with Him.

Under this grace we all benefit from the "get out of jail free card," including the clergy. So when you hear that the bishop was caught on tax evasion, it just means he got caught and we didn't. Many still do not know that you can find all kinds of creative ways to avoid paying taxes, especially if you have a good accountant. But evading your taxes will get you prison time. There is a difference.

Now if it is no t too late and I haven't offended you, please understand: God's purpose for my life is not to insult you or the men or women of God. But please understand that there are those who will read these words and find healing in knowing that the hurts that were exacted against them by the people I am describing was not only toward them but a multitude as well.

I also need to make reference to the majority of men and women in the full time ministry of the Lord and Kingdom building business. These are people who are full of integrity and are upright and respectable

warriors before man and before God. I am merely illustrating the mindset and methodology of those who give them a bad name.

So here's some of the back story with the church. Some of the pastors in full-time ministry are men and women who could not function in corporate America. Many couldn't get up on time and responsibly put in 40 hours at someone's behest while taking direction and criticism. The fact is many of today's pastors couldn't function in your life day to day, yet they preach that we need to hold on to God's unchanging hand. Many of them couldn't hold on, which is why they quit or were fired, several times.

Many of our men and women of God were written up for inappropriate behavior, inappropriate computer use and abuse of privileges if they were in a leadership position. Most couldn't follow the leader if a rope was tied around their wrists. Yet these same preachers admonish us to follow them with almost reckless abandon. Many pastors must be in the spotlight and give the orders because if they were church members they would want to sing all the solos in the choir and sit wherever they wanted and do whatever they wished. Yet these same pastors admonish us to not be this way.

There are many pastors who are true peacocks.

They must look the best, be heard the most and receive the highest level of appreciation; but they tell us to be humble and your gifts will make room for you. Let the church say, *Amen*!!!

There are pastors and ministers who prey on the innocent and vulnerable because they lack the integrity and testicular fortitude to court and attract someone who isn't in a weakened state. There is a phrase for that: it's called a sexual predator. They bring them under their wing and abuse their authority and cause all kinds of damage in the spirit and the flesh.

There are male and female ministers who have passed on or have become untouchable and have never apologized to the people they have hurt. They leave these lives injured and battered along the road side like road kill without any closure or sympathy.

The news headlines you have heard over the years are a mere tip of the iceberg relative to what is actually going on. I promise you that the men and women of God and the politicians and power structure they are tied to will come pummeling down on them and everything they touch. Galatians 6:7 says, *"Be not deceived; God is not mocked: for whatsoever a man soweth, that shall he also reap."*

As sad as it may be, these people do not know

that they are also writing the destiny of their children by their words and actions. The curse may not even fall upon them but upon their offspring or their children's children. This payback will come when they are also vulnerable and in need of kindness. I have seen it with my own eyes.

Imagine coming to one of these ministers for counseling and you bear your bleeding heart to them only to hear your identical situation become the subject of their next sermon from across the pulpit or over the airwaves via TV or radio. Imagine the feeling of vulnerability and betrayal. I have heard pastors threaten people's lives because of business dealings that went south.

Although I could never prove it, I know in my gut that some ministers are at the core of some of the major crimes that take place in some of our urban areas. Some pastors have borrowed money and loaned money with the same care that you would expect from a crack head or a loan shark. Some pastors have entered into business endeavors with the sole purpose of defrauding all but themselves.

Here's a classic example of the predatory instincts of some of our clergy. We've all seen the person or the couple who visit and appear very prosperous. They may be an entertainer, successful business person, athlete or doctor. The pastor swoops in by first taking them to lunch and welcoming them into his or her graces.

This normally begins with giving them the best seat, best parking privileges, best treatment and unfettered access to their office. In essence this new member on the fast track to the right hand of fellowship is getting the kind of favor you were never shown. Or perhaps if you were, it ceased the moment the pastor realized you were not rolling in money. *Don't worry. As soon as the pastor realizes the new flavor of the week isn't wealthy either, they too will mysteriously stop coming to church.*

The difference between them and you is you stuck it out. Hopefully by this point the vipers with the tongues dripping with blood and the penchant for childhood games haven't gotten to you by now. I'm speaking of our fellow church family and lay membership. To thoroughly cover the mindset of church folk overall, it would require another book, but I think you get my point.

CAN ANYONE HEAR ME?

There have been numerous stories about the Catholic Church and the homosexual allegations against their clergy. What we don't hear much about is the evangelical church's multiple scandals on the same along with adultery, fornication, children outside of the marriage and sexual misconduct of every kind despite age, gender and affiliation.

> ***Truth should not offend; if it is truth, it has hit its intended mark.***

The same exists but in smaller proportions in Muslim mosques. Yet, we will never hear how much because of the shame that bringing these allegations would bring upon the victims and the entire community. So these victims are forced to suffer in silence. I am here to tell you that if this is you, there truly is a God. He wants you healed of what was done to you and because He lives, you will draw the strength to forgive. He will seek His vengeance in your honor.

No longer are you supposed to drag your self-esteem around under your belly as you pull yourself through the dirt, looking at the soles of people's feet your whole life; only to be carried by the occasional kindness of others. The God of Abraham sent His only Son and just as He raised Lazarus from the grave, He wants you to get out of your death bed.

He wants you to shake off your grave clothes and not hop but walk boldly before the Master and claim your healing. God loves you enough to have you read these words right now instead of six months ago. God wants you to be like the crippled man lying at the pool of Bethesda

This story took place in the Muslim quarter of Jerusalem. The name Bethesda means "House of Mercy." By this pool would be those who were blind, deaf and crippled. There was a man who was crippled for 38 years and had to crawl or be picked up to get around. He could never get to the pool to get his healing because when the opportunity came for him, someone else got their healing first and he would miss out.

Jesus, the great Physician, came along and told Him to get up and walk with the mat that once held him. He immediately did so and at once he was healed. Jesus knows that you have missed opportunities to get up from your situation. So He has come along through these words Himself to say that it is time to get up and lay down your infirmity.

Don't carry this issue with you another day. The next opportunity may not come for another year. You have to be desperately in need of change to finally drop the stench of pain, resentment and death. I know you're saying that you see the light at the end of the tunnel, but it's not as far away as you think. This is not just about you. God wants to turn your scars into jewels because right now someone is going through exactly what you experienced. They won't receive the testimony from your test from anyone else.

They won't want to hear my story because I didn't experience the same level of detail and circumstances that you endured. That person will only open up as you are opening up and as they sense the delivering Spirit of God in your life. They will need to see the tears and the smile of victory that only you can give them.

Why? Because they are just like you? Get up and put this behind you for the God of salvation who saw you through to this day in spite of the times you pleaded for Him to take your life. Jesus' love and mercy for you knew that here would be better days ahead.

FINDING PURPOSE FOR YOUR BETRAYAL

Some trials come as a result of God simply desiring to brag on us because He knows that we will bring Him glory as we go through trials. There once was a Jewish girl who like so many in her region of the world would follow tradition and sit by the feet of her grandfather and learn of their God of salvation. Things were normal in her life as she grew naturally and in her passion for knowledge of this God. At this point of history a girl was considered a woman by the age of 13 and she would soon be required to wed a man, bear him children and care for her home.

Around the age of 13, God's messenger, the Angel Gabriel, visited Nazareth to see Mary, a virgin who was engaged greeted her and told her to not be afraid. He told her that she will soon be with child and give birth to a son and to call Him Jesus. We all know the story from there. But as in all circumstances in life that change our destiny forever, there is a back story that we don't often stop to ponder.

At first glance, this promise was complete chaos. She was engaged and now had to hurry up and get married before folks started doing the math. The same angel had to visit Joseph, her fiancé, so that he would not cast her away. Mary naturally thought to herself, "Why me and why this way?" But as she felt God's predestined peace, she said "May your word to me be fulfilled," then she sang a song.

As you sit silently in the midst of your storm of stagnation, understand that God is giving you silence to get your attention. Use this time to absorb the favor of God by saying, "Speak, for your servant is listening." (1 Samuel 3:7-11).

Think of it this way: if God permitted you to continue the way you were going, wouldn't you have become one of those who became lovers of themselves? Take courage Mary, there is purpose in your trial. Meditate once again on Luke 10:27-30, *"My sheep listen to my voice; I know them, and they follow me. I give them eternal life, and they shall never perish; no one can snatch them out of my hand. My Father, who has given them to me, is greater than all; no one can snatch them out of my Father's hand. I and the Father are one."*

One day someone will also see the light at the end of the tunnel but they will feel the same spirit of fear that you are feeling now. The light will not be far but between where they are and where you now stand is dark and filled with glass and dangerous debris and they are barefoot and dragging on the ground.

They will see you and Jesus standing behind you beckoning to them. Your voice giving your testimony will be the comfort that will lead them to the Comforter. Listen carefully for the peace of God as it interrupts the chaos that has drained your body daily and gave you restless nights.

This peace promises you an inner embrace that eluded you for so long. The embrace you searched for in a man's eyes but he betrayed you. The embrace from within that you sought after in her eyes but she couldn't hold up her end of the bargain. The embrace from within that urged you to pursue the lifestyle and the people who couldn't live up to your expectations.

> ***Because God pre-programmed your DNA to only accept His original and not man's five-dollar knockoffs. The embrace from within will give you a good night's sleep and the joy that man cannot ever challenge or touch again.***

The hope and anticipation that you seek is actually honing in on you right now like a heat-seeking missile. And the enemy can't do anything about it. By the time you have read this book and we have gotten to know each other better, I will claim your complete healing and restoration to your original factory setting plus the punitive damages that that is owed you for the years that the enemy has defiled, ***In Jesus Name. Amen!!!***

CHAPTER TWO

THE BRUISING PROCESS

Unless the value of something is determined, its abuse is inevitable

Secular humanism dictates that we as human beings represent the highest self. This philosophy espouses reasoning, personal thought and intellect as one's means to reach personal fulfillment. Many atheists and secular humanists utter this phrase at some time or another: "How can such a loving God allow such horrible things to happen to innocent people?" When someone goes through tragedy and is not rooted in a Godly belief system, it is easy for them to adopt this kind of outlook.

The enemy of mankind relishes in these moments. He isolates us in our time of pain and leads us to think that we are all alone, and that life and the God we serve are flawed. He is half right. This life and earth are flawed with the sin his presence brings, but the only advocate we have in this life is the Spirit of the living God—the Holy

Spirit. We may feel that our family and friends will never forsake us, but the enemy can use them to simply not be there when we need someone the most.

Let's face it; people cannot be in all places at all times. What if every fear and anxiety you have ever had in this life reaches across your b d at 2:30 in the morning and attempts to snuff your life away? And the horror won't even let you breathe?

Regardless of whom you are sleeping with or who you feel you can call, the only connection that is built into your soul is the one with Jesus and the Holy Spirit. I have heard from man y in the healthcare field speak of professed atheists who scream the name of Jesus on their death beds and in their darkest hour of need. Their intellect may have them confounded, but their spirit knows where truth lies.

> *Take a moment to understand this: Even in the midst of the chaos and hell that may have or ever will come your way, God will always be in control. Nothing is a surprise to Him. No one ever pulls anything over on Him.*

Time, light and darkness all belong to Him. All life and creational sciences belong to H im. Only God can make the progression of a disease completely revert and return the healing control of a body to itself. There are 100 billion galaxies in the universe and 100 million stars in each galaxy. There are some stars in the universe that can actually hold 500 million suns the size of ours. How many are 100 billion? If we were to count to 250 in a minute, day and night, it would take us about 1,000 years to reach 100 billion.

Perhaps we have a better understanding of the enormity of God when Jesus said *"All authority in heaven and on earth has been given to me."* (Matthew 28:18). In Isaiah 40:12 the prophet said, *"Who has measured the waters in t he hollow of his hand, or with the breadth of his hand marked off the heavens? Who has held the dust of the earth in a basket, or weighed the mountains on the scales and the hills in a balance?"*

If God can fathom the metrics of a universe, He can certainly take hold of the matters that shape the state of affairs going on between your ears. Jesus left us a Comforter who is the person in the Godhead we spend the most time with, yet know the least about. Taking time to understand the Holy Spirit's value to God and His purpose for us is the sole key to any sense of restoration and fulfillment in this life.

By not connecting with our purpose through Him is where we fail to understand the value of anything and anyone in this life. Here is where the bruising process takes place if we don't apply heaping amounts of God's mindset to our wounds.

We are spiritual beings temporarily encased in flesh. Our spirit craves to be released from this flesh and return to God's presence. It's as if you were freshly showered and cleaned up but told that you had to wear someone else's clothes that have been walking the streets without showering for months.

After you woke up from being unconscious for 15 minutes you would be totally disgusted with still having to subject yourself to such humiliation. This is what your spirit feels each time you fail to look for the value of God's wisdom in each experience and each person you encounter.

This behavior is all part of the sinful nature that appalls our spirit. While Jesus walked the earth, He was both humanity and divinity. But even as God in the flesh He became weak at times and had to get alone by Himself so that His divinity could reinforce His humanity for its divine purpose. Otherwise it would be quite easy for Jesus to choose disobedience over obedience to His heavenly Father.

After living in flesh for 33 years, Jesus knew firsthand how difficult living here and trying to be Christ-like can be. That is why He gave us the Holy Spirit to serve as a Counselor, Teacher and

Guide. The purpose of the Holy Spirit is to lead us in the right way and convict us when we fail so that we can go back and make it right.

Without the Holy Spirit's presence in the earth, life would be complete chaos. His presence is what keeps the enemy from completely taking over life on this earth as we know it. The biggest secret to achieving success each day is simply choosing to greet the Holy Spirit in the morning before doing anything else. I will cover this more in depth in the next chapter, "Taking Dominion."

The spirit and the body must work in balance in order for us to take certain cues on how to please the Spirit of God by understanding how the body works. From the moment our body gets injured the vital cells necessary for defense and healing jump into motion. Whether we do the right thing on the outside to mask the long-term effects of an injury, the body is pre-programmed to ward off long-term damage or infection that may compromise the body's ability to function or survive.

Through a series of steps called the immune response, the body summons one (or all) of the three layers to its defense system. We have our skin as a primary defense system, as well as our mucous membranes and our white blood cells.

If these are compromised then the body goes into a mode that will shut down various functions in order to preserve vital organs such as the brain and breathing. When we sustain mental hurt and spiritual attack there are far more variables to consider than simple chemical and motor responses. Our spirituality and psychology are more intricate than the physical and chemical. So therefore we need to take great care in our primary emotional and secondary response to hurt.

When we encounter pain and disappointment, psychologists say we react based on our personalities and instincts for "fight or flight." Some folks stand up and fight for themselves, while others may walk away and think things through and come back for careful discussion or a secondary fight. Then there are those who don't react at all and internalize their pain. Regardless of the style of expression that works for you, the issue that is paramount is the long-term effect on your overall well-being.

I still have a couple of scars on my body from injuries sustained over the years. Some come from burns and scrapes and are faint in my memory as how they occurred. Others are obvious and bring back painful memories. However, although the scars and memories of pain are still there, neither prevents me from functioning in any area of life.

When we look at the bruising process, there are gradual yet progressive steps the body takes toward healing on its own unless predisposed circumstances or new events are introduced that hinder this process.

The mind and the spirit are not nearly as simple. They are almost interconnected in some ways and diametrically opposed in others. For example, a battered woman may have decided that she will not get hit *one more time.* Her mind is made up and her spirit says, *we will not let this break us until we get to a safe place where we can break down.* Then again, when our spirit realizes it's time to let go of the hurt and resentment and move on, our mind may say, "No," because it can't get past the pain.

FIND A CORNER

Have you ever watched a cat or animal get hurt? They run off to a corner where they can either lick their wounds to recoup and fight again another day. Some may use this quiet place to die with dignity. Like that child that gets a tiny cut that stings terribly, they won't let you look at it for fear that you will make it feel worse. They would rather stay there and cry than let you cause them any additional discomfort, even though you are there to help them.

When we suffer an incident that hurt us physically, mentally or both, our immediate reaction may not always be the best.

Accidentally swallowing a corrosive liquid shouldn't be remedied by trying to throw it up. Throwing it up may cause more damage as it tears at the lining in your esophagus on its way up.

Sometimes you have to swallow something that will neutralize the acid. *If the other person had no foul intent, sometimes you may have to swallow your pride and just let it go instead of bringing it all up again and run the risk of causing more damage to yourself.*

If someone did something to you it may require you to go out into the middle of the room and scream so you can draw attention to the perpetrator instead of dying silently in the corner. A rapist or pedophile needs to be exposed and brought to justice where that person can be punished and/or treated for his or her sickness. By you going into the corner to protect yourself, you are also protecting them so they can hurt someone else down the road. The bruising process is also evident when you deny that you are hurting and don't spend any time alone or in the confidence of a trained therapist so that you can get better.

This is where the bruising process may progress to an infection. When you suffer a cut or a bruise, it is recommended that you wash it out and apply an anti-bacterial spray or cream that will serve as a topical agent or shield that will fight bacteria. If you don't take the right steps initially, then an infection will occur. If you don't deal with the hurt your mind has suffered, then you will develop an unhealthy thought process toward that aspect of your life.

If your injury came from a breach of trust, then you will keep yourself from trusting anyone again. This can harm you in a way that costs you the ability to share and receive from others. You will develop false coping and defense systems that aren't even needed. Just because one person abused the privilege of your trust doesn't mean that everyone else will. This may have been the test that would help you graduate to the level of maturity to r eceive and appreciate the next person, someone who may turn out to be the love of your life.

> **God allowed this hurt to prepare you because the love of your life will not be perfect either.**

Now when God sends you someone completely innocent of your past hurts and they want to come into your heart, they will see all the bars on the windows and sense all the tension in your heart. They will now be less likely to relax and want to stay on your terms.

When life's hurts make you come up with enough pre-conditions then you will be viewed as damaged goods. When your damaged goods start to cause enough damage to the populace then it's time to pull the product out of the marketplace—the same way the Department of Agriculture mandates food recalls when there is a risk of food poisoning.

Some bruises will start to look worse before they get better. This does not mean that the body is not progressing on the inside. Sometimes that ugly scar is just a protective bond the body creates so that it can get to work. This process is just temporary and will soon fade and reveal new tissue and complete healing. There still may be a scar, but how well you treat the wound initially will determine the scars you bear for others to see later.

Whichever is your current circumstance, I will share some ideas that will help you put some burn ointment on your mind and soul. This way, any scarring you encounter won't hinder your abilities to move on one day and live pain free.

DAMAGE ASSESSMENT

After a disaster takes place, an investigative team moves in to assess whether there was any malice behind the damage. After the investigative team leaves, insurance adjusters assess the monetary damage and how much it will cost to renovate or rebuild. If you are still alive, there is hope. I am a strong advocate of seeking therapeutic counseling from a qualified Christian or spiritually-grounded counselor. I say this because these individuals offer another dimension to consider in the long run. Namely, how you want your spirit to feel as a result.

Do you want to be the victim or the victor? Please understand that I am not making that statement to be taken likely. There are some people—you and I both know them—who find it challenging to get through the day unless they have something to complain about. Regardless of how wonderful and sweet things are for the rest of the world, they must find a challenge in everything. These people prefer being the victim.

At the point you make a conscious effort to instead be the victor, you desire to see your circumstances differently. There has to be an immediate change that takes place. It's as if a light flickered on in your existence. This light illuminates a portal to your life that you never knew existed. It not only exposes all the dark and ignorant areas of your life, it also brings with it a gust of fresh, cool, aromatic air to flush out and bring life to all the stale and stagnant areas of your thought life.

Choosing to move from victim to victor is not a multi-step method. This is as simple as having to drag yourself through life on your stomach and living a day-to-day existence looking at the soles of people's feet as you drag your body through the streets. That is, until one day someone deliberately approaches you and kneels to your level without the intent of further insulting you.

This person takes you by the hand and says, "Why are you down here? Get up and walk, because this is your privilege." You pause for a moment to digest these sacred words and then stand to your feet. Your posture may take a moment or two to correct, but you will no longer drag your thoughts and existence through life.

As a victor you can now change your thought life from Charlie Brown's lyrics, "Why is everybody always pickin' on me?" to "Nope, try again." The final day of my last job in corporate America represented my last day dragging myself on my stomach. After seeing a therapist, I realized the depression stalking me came from trying to fit my size 14 foot into that corporation's size 10 leadership position.

One day, you may find that the role you are trying to fit is the role that man designated to you instead of the role God created you to fulfill. Stop allowing people to rent space in your head. You as an individual do matter to God. Why else would

He pursue mankind for restoration by sending us a Savior to die as the penalty for the mess we got ourselves into?

YOUR SECRET PLACE

Sometimes after a horrific accident or crime, the crime scene investigators or insurance adjusters need to isolate the scene, known as "sealing" it. In cases of wreckage, the investigators or adjusters may need to move all the wreckage to a controlled setting to further examine or reconstruct the wreckage to better replay the incident. In doing so the proper blame and resolution may be applied so that there can be closure.

When you have sustained a serious hurt in your life you need to do the same thing. If God forbid a small private plane crashes in your backyard and bursts into flames, you won't look out the window and watch it burn itself out. Initially the crash and explosion may stun you, but you will eventually snap into flight or fight mode by calling 911 and seeing if you can safely assist anyone on board. It would be totally unnatural to watch the fire and explosion turn to intense smoke and a smoldering wreck until years later, when it becomes a pile of rusted metal. But that's what many of us do when we encounter personal hurt.

Although people walk by every day and see

the appearance of wreckage in our lives, we pretend that there is nothing to discuss. We shut them out because of our pride and lack of trust. Although pride and trust are walls of defense, they can also cause your life deprivation. When we put this wall up, we keep the search and rescue teams from getting to our aid.

Your secret place is where you can be safe to cry, curse, and scream at the top of your lungs as well as spit and throw things—the same things you did as a kid except now it's with more focus and intent. Doing this initially is acceptable, but continuing three years later is not. After you've expressed your hurt it's time to determine if this is bigger than your faith to allow God to heal you or your ability to reason through it.

Here are some factors to be aware of for finding that secret place.

1. Find somewhere private and away from prying ears and eyes, even if it's in your car in a remote shopping mall parking lot.

2. Eliminate distractions and unnecessary stimuli like television and music with superficial or irrelevant lyrics.

3. Give yourself a consistent, prearranged time even if you think you don't need it. Having the need to take time for self is not

a sign of weakness, but of self-preservation. You can't be there for anyone else if you are no longer here. After a bad case of the flu, your body needs to ease back into its routine. You don't want to cripple your ability to think forward but you don't want to be in d enial either. Use your common sense and victor mentality.

4. Be private about your healing the same way you are about your personal hygiene. Don't draw attention to your time alone so that it remains protected and sacred.

5. Make sure that this secret place is clean and safe so that you are not distracted by circumstances.

Now that you have that place, visit it regularly. Here are some suggested tools to take with you when you go there.

1. Pray for God to clear your mind of distractions and people who are not helpful to your ability to hear Him. Bear in mind that sometimes these people may include you. Get over yourself and all the things that impress you about you. None of them impress God. In fact, they keep Him from getting closer to you. Your status is of no significance to the Creator of all we can think or comprehend.

2. Take courage with you. You will need it to make the necessary changes regarding the healing that needs to take place in your life.

   This may require having to forgive someone who will never say, "I'm sorry."

3. Your Bible. Take a print out of specific scriptures that are related to your pain so that you can recite these scriptures audibly and internalize them. You can find some of these scriptures on my website (www.freedomperspectiveministries.com) or in your Bible's concordance. If you don't have such a section, purchase one that does. When it's time for healing and forgiveness to become the objective, take these scriptures with you and internalize them.

4. A note pad. You will want to take notes of thoughts and wisdom that come to you in this secret place. God may give you an action plan or the words to speak concerning your circumstances to the people concerned.

5. Pictures of your loved ones and some items that bring you peace. *There will come a time in your healing process that keeping focus on the things that matter most is paramount.* Seeing the smiling faces of your children, spouse and other valued family members and friends will keep

you grounded as you chart a course to restoration.

6. If it will help relax you, take along some meditation music. For some, music is an instant tension reliever.

7. Remove excess make-up, jewelry, dress clothing and constrictive clothing. You will be surprised that removing your heels, jackets, neck ties and excess make-up will help you to be more real. You can always re-apply makeup later. However, with it on you will be more concerned about ruining your make-up than getting your breakthrough.

When a trauma patient is rushed into surgery, the first thing the medical staff does is cut through the patient's clothing so that there is no obstruction in the procedure that needs to be done. The more deliberate you are about what you take into this secret place the more focused you will be on healing and getting the job done.

YOUR CONDITION WILL NOT BE YOUR OUTCOME

Your secret place is where you can say things like, "What gave them the nerve to feel they could say or do something like that?" Your secret place is where you can choose to replay the incidents of the wrecks in your life.

Notice that I said the wrecks in your life— not your life, the wreck. I heard a preacher once use the phrase, "Your condition will not be your outcome. Don't allow yourself to be defined by your circumstances." If divorce caused the tearing down of your walls of security, don't refer to yourself as just a divorced individual or a failure.

Encountering wrecks like a divorce simply mean that you now have the experience to bring more to the table. There is a dimension of love, sacrifice and wisdom that you are empowered with, information that someone who has never married can't express. Being divorced will either give you the tenacity to stick it out or the insights to steer clear of the same situation.

People who have perfect lives without a ripples or wrinkles simply don't have a lot to say to someone who has been going through hell. A life without any failures and battle scars is not the life that attracts interest from others. In fact, that kind of life doesn't even sound authentic. A life that has had supposed failures now has the experience to counsel and encourage someone from the seat of experience, not theory. Without a test you have no testimony.

People who have experienced failure and grown from it will tend to have more compassion for those who are now going through the same thing. The counsel I receive from someone who has experienced failure and hurt gives me that edge so that I'll know the "what if" scenario if it occurs. Your life is not your own. You were not created to be an acorn that falls from the tree and rolls aimlessly down the street, only to be stepped on and crushed. As you read on you will grow to understand that there is purpose to everything that God allows you to endure.

Another very wise preacher shared the phrase. "You must accept what God allows." God taught him this in the midst of suffering through the death of his loved one. We may not personally know his pain, but his experience has yielded him the wisdom that he can take with him and share every place he goes. Now the pain he once endured is more distant than the fulfillment he gets from those lives he can help to heal as a result of his experience.

The Lord knows the outcome of every situation before it arises. As every good father does, He wants only the best for us. As children we may have hated homework and tests, but how else would our developing brains get the exercise they needed to fully develop?

Changes come to protect us from stagnation. If a fetus remains in its comfort zone (the womb) too long, the mother's body will begin to attack the unborn child.

To the rest of the world it is unnatural for a baby to still be in the womb at five years of age.

However, the unborn baby would see no problem with it at all. Although birth can be a traumatic time for a baby, its life depends on it. We need to ask the Lord for His perspective on the changes we go through.

> *Change comes to elevate. In order for an elevator to lift, the doors must first close.*

Accepting God's will in our lives is as natural as the mound of clay being made into something of use and value by the Potter's hands. Not accepting God's will is as unnatural as the mound of clay dictating to the potter what it feels it should become. Not all things will be answered now, but time is the ultimate authority on all things, and **time is only accountable to God**. Godly wisdom does not come from man; it is judiciously revealed by God through prayer and His Word, the Bible.

God's reasoning cannot be clipped like a coupon from a Sunday paper. There is no microwaveable solution to what takes real time to achieve. Use this period of your healing to apply time and slow care to your wound. Allow the Lord to show you His hand in the midst of your aftermath. What made Job such a classic case of complete trust in God is that He knew he was not going anywhere, even when his wife and his friends thought he was receiving the wrath of God.

> ***Man will sometimes understand what you are going through, but only the Author of our faith knows why you are going through it. That's why it is said that any man can count the amount of seeds in an apple, but only God knows the amount of apples in one seed.***

This stands to reason that we need to concern ourselves more with the audience of one we have with our God than we have with the concerns and validation of man.

The key to accepting what God allows lies in *"...he leads me beside the still waters **(but if the waters become troubled)** he restores my soul. Even though I walk through the valley of the shadow of death, I will fear no evil **(Oh death where is your sting, Oh grave where is your victory?)** for you are with me, your rod and your staff, they comfort me **(God's got your back)**. You prepare a table before me in the presence of my enemies. **(I shall have peace even in the company of my enemies)** You anoint my head with oil; my cup overflows **(His anointing upon me is more than I'll ever need)**. Surely goodness and love will follow me all the days of my life, and I will* *dwell in the house of the Lord forever." (Psalm 23:2-6, with commentary added).*

God hasn't made a mistake. There is no flaw in His plan concerning you. Feeling this way isn't considered being spiritual, but it certainly is naturally correct. This is normal when you think of it. Once again this is that analogy of the Spirit being imprisoned in our flesh. The two of them need balance or they will be at desperate odds with each other and you will end up living in misery.

The mind's view is to always doubt what it can't understand and the Spirit's purpose is to believe and interpret what the mind can't see. This is called faith. Even the most faithless individuals show faith several times a day. When they go to sleep they believe that their heart will not stop in the middle of the night to cause them sudden death. When they take a seat in a chair, they expect that it will support their weight.

They don't pick the chair up and inspect it with a flashlight and an instruction manual to justify its structural integrity. They just plop their rump down and conduct business as usual. So, you see, even our mind's methodology is flawed. In the next chapter, "Taking Dominion," I will review the methodology of the enemy and how he uses these tactics to strike fear and doubt in your life. The Lord will show you how to use the

Holy Ghost in your speech and thought process daily in order to give the enemy a panic attack every time you open your mouth.

Unless the value of something is determined, its abuse is inevitable. It is man's sinful nature to abuse things that he doesn't understand. Most of us have never been taught our value, so therefore we abuse our bodies, our spirits, and our minds. We give free reign for others to do the same. In the next chapter you will learn how to use your secret place to run an appraisal of your life. In order to know your greatness, you need to know the greatness of Him who made you.

Let me put this another way. ***Your season will not become your climate***. Seasons change but a climate is determined by several years of sustained and consistent weather conditions. These conditions are gathered scientifically and studied for years before a determination is made as to what the climate is. So don't rush to conclusion about your life being seen as what you are made to feel.

My purpose is to help you serve the enemy his eviction papers from your life. It's time to turn your life around so that he takes his God-assigned position, beneath your feet. The enemy is subject to you and you are supposed to have dominion over him and every one of his manifestations. It's time to take back everything you allowed him to take. Far too long too many believers have been like three - year -olds, crying for the lollypop he stole. Now it's time to go at him the way Mike

Tyson used to go at his opponent in the ring. It's time to strike fear in the spiritual realm of this world by stirring up the atmosphere with the knowledge of your priestly inheritance.

Are you ready? Let's do it!

CHAPTER THREE
TAKING DOMINION

Those whom the Lord called were predestined to achieve greatness before the foundations of the world were framed with these words: "Let there be." So therefore before you apply your faith to the spirit realm for acceptance; just know your approval was already on its way.

THE THOUGHT PROCESS

One of my favorite axioms is by an unknown writer:

> *"Watch your thoughts, for they become your words; watch your words, for they become your actions; watch your actions, for they become your habits; watch your habits, for they become your character; watch your character, for they become your destiny."*

If one out of five people on this planet truly understood and followed this methodology, this world would have a 20 percent chance of being a better place to live. That estimation is my goal and by the end of this book, I pray it will become your goal as well. If you're not already a believer of this methodology, let's start by disciplining you. Your thoughts and your thought process are the most private thing you own. Even your salvation is something you have to share and speak of if you are following the great commission:

"Then Jesus came to them and said, 'All authority in heaven and on earth has been given to m e. Therefore go and make disciples of all nations, baptizing them in the name of the Father and of the Son and of the Holy Spirit, and teaching them to obey everything I have commanded you. And surely I am with you always, to the very end of the age.'" (Matthew 28:18-20)

The only thing that is purely private is your thoughts. If someone stole your wallet or pocketbook they may use you credit cards and I.D. and assume your identity, but they can't assume your thoughts. Your thoughts, the most intimate part of your existence, tell the true story about who you really are.

These thoughts speak the truth about everybody you know, meet and love. They even

speak the truth about your feelings about God.

So in order to transform your life from victim to victor, you must first be able to transform your thought processes.

Aren't you glad that we don't wear our thoughts on our forehead for the entire world to see? One third of us would likely be in jail. Another third would be friendless and loveless. The other third would be on the run or in seclusion, wearing ski caps. This illustrates the raw power of our intent, words and actions. These are the original triple threat. God said, "Let us make man in Our image" (Genesis 1:26), which shows His intent. God said "Let there be light" (Genesis 1:3) demonstrates His words. And "So God created man in His own image" (Genesis 1:27), His actions. You see, God literally framed the universe, planned mankind and then did it.

Do you not see the awesome power that God can express through you? If the enemy could pick ten scriptures in the Bible he hates the most, I'm sure one of them would be, (Luke 10:19) *"I have given you authority to trample on snakes and scorpions and to overcome all the power of the enemy; nothing will harm you."*

This is the scripture that would render the enemy's kingdom futile if we as believers truly understood and "bought into" God's intent by having Jesus articulate this. The enemy has this world so bent on self-pleasure and distraction from God's Word that we conveniently overlook the things that bring us abundant life. We need to take on the mind of God in order to capture His favor and power in our lives.

Philippians 2:5 (KJV) says, *"Let this mind be in you, which was also in C hrist Jesus..."* Jesus wants us to have his mind. What kind of mind is that? Examine the preceding four verses: *"If there be therefore any consolation in Christ, if any comfort of love, if any fellowship of the Spirit, if any bowels and mercies, fulfill ye my joy, that ye be likeminded, having the same love, being of one accord, of one mind. Let nothing be done through strife or vainglory; but in lowliness of mind let each esteem others better than themselves. Look not every man on his own things, but every man also on the things of others."*

What is the mind of God? God wants us to occupy our thoughts with love and selflessness. In order to accomplish this, He tells us, *"Be ye transformed by the renewing of your mind."* (Romans 12:2, KJV). The Greek word for renewing is *anakainosis*, which means *detoxify* and *restore*. So God is not saying to just simply change your mind. He is saying to renovate it by detoxifying your mind, removing poisonous thoughts and ways that slowly kill.

It is a harsh fact to accept that *some* of the things that have happened in our life have occurred because of the words we spoke and thoughts we harbored. The laws of attraction come into play, regardless of how much a Christian or a sinner you are.

Let's take a moment here and reflect on that. In order to achieve the changes we want in our lives, we must embrace that first we need to make some of the biggest changes within ourselves. You can literally have a changed life while reading this book, not simply because I wrote it and I want to get credit.

I get the credit for nothing. If you decide to change, it will be because the truths assembled in these pages are set forth in this season of your life, and that you are ready to accept them because of your maturity and brokenness. Every revolution that has ever taken place came about through a combination of desperation and timing.

Your maturity is timing and your brokenness comes from being tired of the same. This revolution from within will only occur if you have total buy-in to the realization that you may not be all that God expects for you to be *toward* Him at this stage of your life.

If you are desperate for change, you must be equally desperate for swapping the thought processes that reaped hurt and disappointment for the identity of Christ. He didn't die for you to take the wheel and cause the wreck you walked away from. He died so that you would soar above the traffic jam that consumes so many others.

"He who dwells in the shelter of the Most High will rest in the shadow of the Almighty." (Psalm 91:1). God wants to be your covering, spokesperson, body guard, big brother, rich and powerful father, husband, and—when needed—the thick emollient that coats your body and fills your every need.

So as we move forward you must understand that the Holy Spirit is a priceless asset. Too many people overlook Him. As a result, they live as poor people, beneath their privilege. As we move forward we will unlock the tools together to summon the inherent, God-given power from the Holy Spirit and take back everything we allowed the enemy to steal from us.

AWARENESS

While He was still on this earth, Jesus told His disciples, *"And I will pray the Father, and he shall give you another Comforter, that he may abide with you forever; even the Spirit of truth."* (John 14:16-17, KJV). Just before He departed, He promised, *"But you will receive power when the*

Holy Spirit comes on you" (Acts 1:8).

There is nothing God wants for us more than that we be successful and happy in this journey until He returns. As any concerned parent who needs to temporarily leave their children, He has made sure He has left us with guidelines (the Bible) and a qualified and responsible Guide (the Holy Spirit) to ensure that we follow them accordingly.

This Guide is powerful—the power is the same Spirit of God that was present when God said to Him, *"Let us make man in our image."* (Genesis 1:26). This Comforter, as Jesus called Him, is the Spirit of God. In fact God esteems this Comforter in a way that He doesn't even speak of Jesus, His Son: "I tell you the truth, all the sins and blasphemies of men will be forgiven them. But whoever blasphemes against the Holy Spirit will never be forgiven; he is guilty of an eternal sin." (Mark 3:28-29).

God is serious about His Spirit. We can't treat the Holy Spirit as a family member or others in our lives that we may choose to address as we pass by them in the hallway. The Holy Ghost is the person in the triune Godhead that we hear the least about even though we spend the most time with Him. *Although He gets us rapture-ready, we know little about Him.* After reading the four gospels, you may have come to the conclusion that the disciples that Jesus chose were a pretty dysfunctional group of men. They had egos, attention-deficit issues, frequent bouts with lethargy, copious amounts of cowardice, and were judgmental and driven by personal gain.

This all brings to mind the personality profile of the modern-day church. This is why the church has not budged from where He left it over 2,000 years ago. The disciples had the excuse of living with God incarnate and not having the advantage of having Him within. What's our excuse? Jesus said we would receive power when the Holy Spirit comes on us.

Do you feel that power? You will. The reason that the modern-day Bible does not have much reference to the Holy Spirit is because when the King James Version was completed in 1611 for the Church of England, the Anglican Church wanted a version more suitable for their leadership structure.

These leaders saw no need for the ambiguity of the Holy Spirit in this new version. The original version was considered "troublesome" to the Puritans. As you may know, the Bible as we know it is far from the complete works of the divinely-inspired Word of God. The missing scriptures have been burned, stolen, and hidden for hundreds of years. Some were found in the Judean desert in the 1940's and speak to the establishment of the second temple, which was the crowning achievement of King Solomon. The rest is left to scholars, archaeologists and great story tellers.

Suffice it to say that the Holy Spirit is here to fill in the blanks. This is why Christ told His disciples, *"I have much more to say to you, more than you can now bear. But when he, the Spirit of truth, comes, he will guide you into all truth. He will not speak on his own; he will speak only what he hears, and he will tell you what is yet to come. He will bring glory to me by taking from what is mine and making it known to you. All that belongs to the Father is mine. That is why I said the Spirit will take from what is mine and make it known to you."* (John 16:12-15).

The Holy Spirit is here to advise, protect and convict us to as we press toward the mark of the high calling which is in Christ Jesus. Now here are the rules of engagement as to how to benefit from this power. The Holy Spirit is the Protector and Sentinel who lives within and never slumbers or fails us if we don't grieve Him.

RULES OF ENGAGEMENT

The Holy Spirit knows what is coming our way beyond our next breath or from around the corner. As we sleep, there are spiritual forces and wickedness that seek to stifle our lives and extinguish our purpose before we awake. We need to understand that God and the Holy Spirit have assigned angels to aid through every waking hour. Psalms 91:11 says, *"For he will command his angels concerning you to guard you in all your ways."*

The enemy doesn't want you to know this. He wants you to wake up and curse God and this day, which you have been given as a gift. He wants you to labor under the same dark and heavy spirit he tried to put on you the day before. There are literally angels waiting for you, ready to he lp you. The Holy Spirit is standing within, awaiting your clean- hearted requests.

These angels can go forth in the day and place your resume on t op of the pile of other applicants. They can soften the heart of the judge, police officer, teacher, boss or whomever else seemingly holds your fate—and those of your loved ones—in his hand.

The Holy Spirit wants to tell you how to react

and what to say when you have no idea of what to do. The Holy Spirit will even advise you on how to pray and what to pray for, but you have to ask Him. Do you want to hear more? Well, there is a catch to having unfettered access to this power. You must first clean up your mind and thought process: "Do not conform any longer to the pattern of this world, but be transformed by the renewing of your mind. Then you will be able to test and approve what God's will is--his good, pleasing and perfect will." (Romans 12:2).

Most see this as a basic request to simply try not to be confused with sinners in the way they think. Here is an in-depth perspective of the Godly version of renewing your mind. The Greek word for *transformed* is *metamorfo*, which is where we get the word metamorphosis. The literal Greek translation is to transfigure, as in the transfiguration of Christ as reviewed in Luke 9:27-36. This is when Jesus was on a mountain and appeared radiant and angelic in appearance as His divinity appeared above the images of Moses and Elijah, the pre-eminent figures of Judaism.

Romans 12:2 is saying to become transformed as in radiance like the Lord. The Greek for the word *renew* is *anakainosis* (pronounced an-ak-ah'-ee-no-sis). The translation for this word is to be completely changed by the removing of impurities—another example of detoxing from deadly poisons. In essence, this verse is saying,

"Stop thinking like the trends of this world; be radiant like Christ inwardly by removing the toxic ways you are thinking.

Then you will be able to see a godly perspective in everything you experience." This kind of outlook will assure success. God's Word was never intended to be a dry history book, but the living Word. Through the pursuit of the Holy Spirit, when you take the time to understand it, you will understand what God intends for your life, personally.

I suggest the best way to start your day in this pursuit of the Spirit of God—for blessings, protection and guidance—is to greet Him properly and fellowship with Him throughout the day. The following is a "Holy Spirit Morning Greeting" that the Lord gave me for the Life Enhancement Classes that I teach.

Memorize and internalize this prayer. Say it immediately as you awake in the morning. Before you greet your spouse or get out of bed, tell the Holy Spirit, "Good morning." Remember that your internal clock didn't wake you, nor did your alarm clock or your spouse. The Spirit of God caused your eyes to open on this side of glory. Greeting Him as such gives Him the glory first for your life.

Holy Spirit Morning Greeting

Lord I thank you this moment for the breath of life and the use of my faculties and my health. This very moment Lord I thank You for your protection in my life from every entity, attempt and manifestation that is unlike You.

Holy Spirit, You are the only Lord of this world. Completely take over my thoughts, my words and my deeds. Because of You, there is nothing that can come into my life physically, mentally or spiritually that can harm me or the lives I love and touch. My desire is to glorify You this day. In Jesus name, Amen!

I purposely placed this prayer in a larger font so that you will have no difficulty finding it on this page should you ever have need of it in a hurry. This is how the Holy Spirit is positioned in our life. He is placed in this earth to be the biggest and most integral person in our lives, but yet we lose Him among too many other (mainly earthly) details of our lives.

Share His glory with other loved ones by logging on to www.freedomperspectiveministries.com. Go to the tab titled "prayers" and print it. Place copies on your bathroom mirror, in your children's bathroom, by your door, in your office and wherever else you need to be reminded of WHO should truly keep your calendar.

ACCEPT THE FACTS

> *Truth merits no reward, nor does it dignify a response. Truth is supreme and therefore absolute.*

When we internalize this reality, then changing one's self and accepting the world as it is around us becomes easier. Here is a list of some items in our lives to take into perspective as we prepare the platform for taking dominion in our lives.

- **Your thought life.** Keep a clean vessel. Just as we find dirty and smelly public restrooms offensive, a toxic thought life can offend the Holy Spirit. You would not dream of spending the night in one of these restrooms, so why should we subject the Holy Spirit to our minds while they are in this state?

- **Watch your mouth.** Our tongue responds directly to the thoughts and intents that drive it. So if our thoughts are filthy, our words will eventually spill out this way. How can we kiss our loved ones, utter words of healing and love and worship, and praise God if our mouths are filthy? You won't drink out of a cup that you found in restroom, would you? Then why would you use that filthy mouth to love on God? As Matthew 12:36-37 says, *"But I tell you that men will have to give account on the* *day of judgment for every careless word they have spoken. For by your words you will be acquitted, and by your words you will be condemned."*

- **Drop the weights that hold you back.** Your perceived strengths may be the things that are actually holding you back. Like many others, we hide behind masks. Transform and renew. If God made you the beauty that you are, then ask Him to show you how He sees you. Get out from behind the heavy makeup, sarcasm, coldness, pride and arrogance. Although life may have made you this way, there are things you must let go of in order to move forward. (Read Judges 6-8). The false weaponry and armor we hide behind will fail us in our battles. Trust God t o prune your excess branches and shed the excess baggage.

4. **Be single and complete.** Just because you are single does not mean you shouldn't be complete. My book, *Single and Complete* covers this in more detail. Don't wait for someone to come along to make you whole. What if they are happy with themselves when they meet your incomplete self? Where does that leave you? God wants to be the One who completes you. He wants to be the One to fill all the cracks and holes. If you allow a man or

woman to do this, then another person will get your love and devotion. Eventually when this other person fails you, you will get mad at God for allowing this to happen.

5. **Beware of haters.** The only person who has ever died for you and rose again is Jesus. As

long as you plan on getting your life together, there will always be those who will come like vultures on fresh road kill. They want to eat up your joy and purpose because they have none of their own. Haters take pleasure in seeing people fall. They never have anything good to say about anyone's success. So be mindful of whom you share your blessings and intent with; they may try to abort your baby.

6. **Balance givers and takers.** Just like waves at the beach, people either bring in or take out. People in our lives are either givers or takers. Beware that you are not surrounding yourself with too many takers at any one time. Also make sure that you don't surround yourself with only givers; this will mean that you are the taker. Life and relationships are all about balance.

7. **Fear's methodology.** The enemy uses fear to distract us from the truth: *I have given you authority to trample on snakes and scorpions and to overcome all the power of the enemy;*

nothing will harm you." (Luke 10:19). Fear of being broke, fear of being alone, fear of not having someone around you, fear of what people would think and say, and fear of not knowing the outcome are the basic fears that hold us back. Well, I've got news for you: people are thinking and talking already, you just haven't heard them yet. The other circumstances can all happen in one day. Remember, fear is not of the Lord but of the enemy.

8. **Exercise discipline, restraint and commitment.**
Discipline: Know when to do the right thing and do it even when you don't feel like it. Restraint: Know when not to do something or withhold from doing that which is not beneficial. Commitment: Do it on a consistent basis, faithfully, so that you will be considered reliable and synonymous with that thing that you do. These words will earn you respect with all who know you, including your haters.

9. **Remember that your past is not your future, nor is your condition your outcome.** Know that all things work together for those who love God and are called according to His purpose (see Romans 8:28). If you know that your thoughts and life are clean, then the hell you went through is supposed to bring everyone you touch a little closer to heaven.

10. **Maybe you are failing the test**. By you remaining or by you being visited by the same cycle of failures or frustrations could be a road sign that you are going in circles. Constant failure in your finances, relationships or social or professional occurrences could mean you are failing to meet the grade. Try to look at

each storm or season as an assignment allowed by God. Each assignment has a list of tasks that you must successfully complete and pass in order to move on. Just like grade school; you must complete various assignments, pass crucial tests and then pass the final examination in order to move up.

It could be possible that you are not moving because you have not asked the Lord to reveal the assigned tasks you must complete in this season. Perhaps He has already shown you but you have just been stubborn about changing your ways.

Maybe He expects more of you in terms of vocalizing your faith to others or more study time in the word. It could be that He wants less murmuring and more rejoicing in the fact that He is Risen and He is Lord. There should be no pre-condition for remaining in a genuine and consistent state of praise and thanksgiving.

> ***So change your perspective and look at some of your storms as a direct result of something that must be changed in you.***

Jesus doesn't want you to lack, He wants you to thrive. (John 10:10 NKJV) ... *I have come that they may have life, a nd that they may have it more abundantly.*

Now that we have some basic ideologies in order, let's put some arms and legs to our form. Now that we know that we need to c lean our minds, what do we substitute for those old thoughts? *Diets aren't just difficult to follow because we know what things we shouldn't eat, they're difficult to follow because we fail to embrace the healthy substitute.* So here is something to wrap your head and words around.

DECLARATIONS

I got my world rocked while teaching the teens one night at my home church. My pastor was away and asked me to fill in for him. I taught on the topic, "No More Fear." I asked the teens to anonymously write down three things: 1) the worst thing you have ever thought, 2) the worst thing you have ever said, 3) the worst thing that you have ever done. Then I collected the papers and mixed them together. The purpose was to illustrate that the enemy has a way of making us think that we are the only one who feels the way we do.

Then I read them aloud so the teens would hear their thoughts read by someone else, as well as understand that they were not alone in their thoughts and actions. Of the 55 I read, only a few weren't about thoughts of murder, suicide, or hatred of their parents. These were suburban kids in a city of about 40,000 people, not gang bangers or kids who have been in and out of jail. This

taught me a valuable lesson about the issues and spiritual attack that all teens and children face on a 24/7 basis.

Daily declarations are an important part of our daily spiritual diet. Like any diet, if we don't consume that which is healthy, our body will suffer in the long run. The same is true of our soul. I captured some of these in my first book *The Power of Perspective*, in a chapter on building a stronger relationship with your child and adolescent.

That night I gave the teens the same declarations I've created in my Power of Perspective book and for my children and was equally blown away by their reaction after they read them aloud. It seemed as though no one had ever told them these things before. As a result of this exercise, I was inspired to ask our pastor to share these same declarations with the entire church, so they could pass them on to their children.

I have also created some affirmations specifically for you. It is important especially for children to be able to focus and meditate on the things of God from an early age. These thoughts will help combat the distractions and destructive thoughts that come into play as they reach adolescence. The devil bombards this age group with these thoughts in an attempt to get them to self-destruct.

These affirmations are designed to keep our minds focused on the things of God as we move through our busy days filled with distractions. Just as you would stand up and stretch your muscles after being in one position for a long period of time, you should do the same for your spirit. Stretch your spirit and mind by reciting these declarations audibly so that your mind can hear the words coming out of your mouth.

These affirmations as well as the Holy Spirit Morning Greeting are all a part of my family's daily devotion time. They have been a blessing to us. These affirmations are also on my website for you to download and include in your environment.

NO MORE FEAR

LORD, I THANK YOU FOR MY LIFE, MY HEALTH, MY PROTECTION AND MY MIND. I THANK YOU FOR EACH DAY OF LIFE THAT YOU BLESS ME WITH THE ABILITY TO THINK ON MY OWN, DRESS MYSELF, WASH AND FEED MYSELF.

FATHER, I PROFESS THAT YOU ARE THE ONLY WISE AND TRUE GOD IN MY LIFE. THERE IS NO GOD IN MY LIFE ABOVE YOU. YOU ARE THE AUTHOR AND

FINISHER OF MY FAITH. LORD, YOU ARE FIRST IN MY LIFE

YOU SAID IN ISAIAH 54:17 THAT NO WEAPON FORMED AGAINST ME SHALL PROSPER. AND, THAT EVERY TONGUE THAT SHALL RISE UP AGAINST ME IN JUDGMENT I SHALL HAVE THE AUTHORITY TO CONDEMN.

I DECLARE THAT MY LIFE IS A MIRACULOUS EXPRESSION OF YOUR LOVE, YOUR HEALING, YOUR FORGIVENESS AND LOVINGKINDNESS. I AM YOUR CROWNING ACHIEVEMENT.

LORD, YOU HAVE MADE ME TO BE

INTELLIGENT, CARING, LOVING, FORGIVING, UNDERSTANDING AND MERCIFUL TOWARD OTHERS. AS A RESULT, INTELLIGENCE, CARING, LOVING KINDNESS, FORGIVENESS, UNDERSTANDING AND MERCY WILL ALWAYS BE SHOWN TOWARD ME.

I DECLARE THAT YOU WILL SURROUND ME WITH YOUR PEACE AND FAVOR. YOU WILL SURROUND ME WITH FRIENDSHIPS AND RELATIONSHIPS THAT M EAN ME WELL AT ALL TIMES.

YOU SAID IN PSALMS 91:11 THAT YOU WILL GIVE ANGELS CHARGE OVER ME TO ACCOMPANY, DEFEND AND PRESERVE ME IN ALL MY WAYS AS LONG AS I AM OBEDIENT. IN THE NAME OF JESUS, I INSTRUCT ALL MESSENGER ANGELS TO MOVE ON MY BEHALF BY WAY OF SPEAKING ON MY BEHALF.

IN THE NAME OF JESUS I DECLARE THAT THE HOLY SPIRIT WILL EMPLOY ALL ANGELIC HOSTS AND E ARTHLY RESOURCES TO GUARANTEE MY SAFE TRAVELS AND MY ABILITY TO ATTAIN AND ACT UPON GOD'S WISDOM, KNOWLEDGE AND UNDERSTANDING

FOR MY LIFE.

IN THE NAME OF JESUS, THESE ANGELIC HOSTS AND EARTHLY RESOURCES WILL PROTECT AND CAUSE ME AND MY LOVED ONES TO PROSPER SPIRITUALLY, MENTALLY AND PHYSICALLY.

HOLY SPIRIT, I KNOW YOU WILL BLOCK THE ENEMY AND THOSE AROUND ME WHO ENVY ME AND WISH ME HARM. YOU WILL CAUSE THE ENEMY TO FAIL IN EVERY ATTEMPT TO M ANIFEST THEMSELVES IN MY LIFE.

HOLY SPIRIT, AS MY COMFORTER I DECLARE THAT YOU ARE THE HEAD OF EVERYTHING I AM AND C AN EVER COMPREHEND. HOLY SPIRIT, GO B EFORE ME IN MY DAILY EXPERIENCES, MY STUDIES, AND MY TEST TAKING ABILITIES.

CAUSE MY MIND TO B E FREE FROM DISTRACTIONS OF ANY KIND AND ANY MANIFESTATION OF EVIL AND DISOBEDIENCE. AS A R ESULT, HOLY SPIRIT, RENEW AND C OMPLETELY RESTORE MY THOUGHTS AND MY PERSPECTIVE TO MATCH YOURS. TEACH ME TO SEE THINGS AND PEOPLE THE WAY

YOU DO, BECAUSE I LOVE YOU THAT MUCH.

LORD, I DECLARE THAT YOU WILL PROTECT MY HOME, MY FAMILY AND EVERYTHING YOU HAVE GIVEN ME. LORD I DECLARE THAT YOUR FAVOR, GRACE AND MERCY SHALL FOLLOW ME EVERYWHERE I GO NOW AND ALWAYS.

IN JESUS NAME. AMEN!!!

DECLARATIONS OF INTENT

FATHER, IN THE NAME OF JESUS, I DECLARE THAT YOU ARE THE ONLY LIFE GOVERNING BEING THAT I WILL ACCEPT INTO MY LIFE.

LORD, THIS VERY MOMENT I SURRENDER MY THOUGHT PROCESSES AND MENTAL FACULTIES TO YOU COMPLETELY. I SURRENDER MY UNGODLY THOUGHT LIFE OVER TO YOU. I PLACE THEM AT YOUR FEET FOR THEIR COMPLETE AND UTTER DESTRUCTION.

FATHER, I DECLARE THAT THROUGH YOUR HEALING AND REDEMPTIVE BLOOD THAT I AM NO LONGER HELD CAPTIVE TO THE EVIL WAYS OF MY PAST. I

SURRENDER THE FIREY, BLOODTHIRSTY HABITS OF MY MOUTH AT YOUR FEET.

LORD, I KNOW THAT MY WAYS ARE NOT PLEASING TO Y OU, SO THEREFORE I OFFER MY BODY, MY TOTAL EXISTENCE AND MY SINFUL CRAVINGS AND SELF-PLEASING HABITS TO YOU S O YOU CAN TRANSFORM AND RENEW ME.

FATHER, PLEASE EMPTY MY CUP OF ANY SINFUL RESIDUE THAT REMINDS YOU OF ME. LORD, TAKE PLEASURE IN THE FACT THAT THE ONLY REFELECTION YOU CAN SEE IN MY CUP IS THAT OF YOU.

LORD, REMOVE ALL DESIRE FOR SINFUL PLEASURES FROM MY LIFE. COMPLETELY REMOVE THE T ASTE FOR THIS SIN FROM MY LIFE SO THAT I T IS NO LONGER FAMILIAR TO ME.

LORD, I KNOW THAT THROUGH YOU I CAN DISPLAY DESCIPLINE, RESTRAINT AND COMMITMENT IN MY WALK WITH YOU. LORD, THROUGH YOUR HOLY SPIRIT I WILL WALK IN A TRUTHFUL PATH AND WILL BECOME BLIND AND IMPERVIOUS TO DISTRACTIONS AND THE FIERY DARTS OF THE ENEMY.

HOLY SPIRIT, THROUGH YOUR

EMPOWERMENT I WILL TURN DOWN MY PLATE FROM EATING TO EXC ESS THE FOODS THAT ARE DAMAGING TO MY BODY AND THEREFORE HARMFUL TO YOUR TEMPLE AND MY ABILITY TO SERVE YOU IN MIND, BODY AND SOUL. HOLY SPIRIT, REMOVE MY URGES FOR THE SUGARS, FATS AND OTHER FOODS THAT SLOWLY DESTROY ME.

LORD, I DECLARE AND DECREE THAT YOU HAVE EMPOWERED ME WITH THE ABILITY TO CLEAN MY MIND AND M Y MOUTH OF THE LANGUAGE AND TH OUGHTS THAT DEFILE YOU.

HOLY GHOST, THROUGH YOUR POWER I HAVE THE AB ILITY TO C OMMAND THE ENEMY TO TAKE HIS HANDS OFF OF EVERY THINGS THAT YOU HAV E GIVEN ME. I NOW HAVE TH E POWER TOFRUSTRATE THE PLANS OF THE ENEMY IN MY LIFE CONCERNING MY PURPOSE.

Obviously, these affirmations can be used in whole or in part. The most important point is that you have words that are Word-inspired to encourage your heart and motivate your walk with the Holy Spirit.

TAKING DOMINION

There comes a time when you've got to show all concerned in your life what you are made of. You need to reveal to God and His angelic hosts, yourself, and the devil your spiritual make-up. Here is an example of showing the enemy of all creation that his eternal fate still lies in Revelations 20:10, *"And the devil that deceived them was cast into the lake of fire and brimstone, where the beast and the false prophet are, and shall be tormented day and night for ever and ever."*

Here is a simple prayer you can internalize that will help empower you when you need a remembrance of who is in charge of whom:

Father God, in the name of Jesus, I come against every power and principality that is unlike Your power. Satan, in the name of Jesus, I come against your every manifestation in my life. I come against the trickery and witchcraft of the spirit of depression, anxiety and fear, and any other mental illness that you use in your bag of tricks and weaponry to attack me. Through the blood of Jesus Christ, I command you to step back from my life and everything and everyone I love and touch. In the name of Jesus, I command you to loose your hold on my clarity of thought and ability

to articulate and express my love and passion for the only wise and true God of this universe, Jesus Christ.

My past is not my future, nor is my condition my outcome. In the name of Jesus, I subvert and come against every plan and tactic that you have orchestrated against me and my life. As a result of the blood shed for me on Calvary, I remand you and every spoken word and desire against me to the foundations of hell from where they have come.

You are the author of all lies and confusion. Every work and word of yours is seeded with death and your imminent destruction. You cannot create life, you can only mimic it. So, therefore, I take authority through the blood of Jesus to remind you of your ultimate destiny, which is already prepared for you in the lake of fire where you will be tormented by unthinkable suffering day and night for all of eternity.

This is the beginning process of how to take dominion over your life. Read these chapters over and over until you are able to apply their relevance to your life on a consistent basis. You will need to be faithful over chapter 3 in order to accomplish chapter 4. Remember, faith without works is dead.

CHAPTER FOUR
THE FORGIVING PROCESS

Choosing not to forgive and letting it go is like drinking poison and waiting for the person who hurt you to die.

PENNIES FOR YOUR THOUGHTS

*I*magine holding on to three pennies all day long and being told that you cannot let go of them. (Period). A penny has the smallest denominational value of any coin minted in an English-speaking country. It makes up 1/100th of the U.S. dollar and is c omprised of zinc and copper, which has little intrinsic value. Here is how this simple piece of metal can cost you everything you own, including your peace of mind.

You will hold these pennies between the index finger and the thumb of your dominant hand. Although the pennies are small and not very heavy, you will eventually feel the strain and inconvenience of having to hold one hand or at least two fingers in a set position as you try to go on with life.

As a force of habit, you will occasionally try to reach for or grasp something with that hand. However, as a result of your inability to hold anything else, you must compensate, over-compensate or accept that you cannot hold on to one thing and receive another.

This inability becomes your disability and eventually a mindset. In time, it will become your lifestyle and destiny. In fact, the value of these pennies may never match the value of the opportunities you have to miss or let go.

> ***Your coping mechanism and mindset will cause you to turn a blind eye to opportunities right in front of you.***

Hopefully, you can see the parallel: your inability to forgive will cloud your judgment and devalue your life. Now do y ou see how three pennies can cost you so much? In grasping tightly to things of little value, you can miss out on job opportunities, relationships, and friendships.

Although you may be able to complete most of your tasks, you will spend every waking moment planning how to accommodate your handicap. Most people will notice something peculiar about you, but won't be able to quite put a finger on it. In holding these pennies, you must also go to sleep without loosening your grip.

If you let go of them, when you get up you will have to immediately locate them. After a period of time you will find yourself seeing a specialist to try to fix the long-term damage for your hand's inability to grasp.

This is how resentment slowly invades the balance and normalcy of our lives. God may need you to take hold of something new, but you can't because your hand is full of something petty.

You see, what you are holding is of no value to the Master. He sent His Son to relieve you of that burden. When we choose to hold onto things like hurt, anger, rage or shame, there is some part of our consciousness that must remember to grip it tightly day and night. Everyone you attempt to be intimate with or maintain a healthy relationship with will feel the burden in your spirit. Your spirit and personality will have to conform to remember to hold on to this little thing. Whether you realize it or not, holding on to something, no matter how small, consumes energy.

Considering that these pennies in one way or another have touched every facet of your life, their appraisal value has the potential to g o through the roof. The purpose of being spiritual beings is not to carry or become obstructed but to be free of burdens and to be transparent before God. I know you probably feel that what you are holding is more serious than a few pennies. You are right. I promise to try to help you see differently by the end of this chapter. In the meantime, try to r emember the only person telling you to hold onto these pennies is you.

I'M STUCK

Most of us have been taught the concept that when someone hurts or offends us that the burden of responsibility for reconciliation falls on the offender. He or she is supposed to sincerely apologize; then we take time to consider the apology so we can decide to forgive them on our terms.

This belief system may vary, depending on the size and severity of the offense. You will notice a stark difference between someone saying, "I'm sorry" when they accidentally bump into you in a crowded shopping aisle or carelessly back into your car outside, compared to an unthinkable act that changed your life forever.

With the exception of the minor offenses I just mentioned, we rarely stop to consider that the burden to forgive becomes heavier to the one offended than the one who caused the offense. The burden says that I must give up my right to hold this offense over another person's head.

As the one doing the forgiving, you must be willing to forego feeling resentment toward the offender. There is a greater degree of difficulty to forgive if the offender shows no remorse for the offense; or, if he or she is no longer alive or it is impossible to get hold of the person to clear the air.

When I say "clear the air," I mean to express your thoughts and feelings about what that person did. Sometimes this forum for *blowing off steam* to the person is almost as cathartic as them coming to you with a sincere, heart-wrenching apology. This helps bring closure so you can move on.

Now that I've said that, none of this would mean a thing if you feel that holding this person accountable is the only justice you can obtain for the hot dagger they've placed in your stomach. While teaching a class on forgiveness, a female student told me, *"If I simply forgive them it would be as if they got away with murder. At least when they see the look in my eye, they feel guilty. I know it because they try to hide or look down."*

While speaking to a single women's ministry, another woman approached me and said me, *"It's hard to forgive my ex because I see him at least twice a week and he is just as smug as he ever was. He doesn't even seem to care that he did me wrong."*

In both cases I hear the same message. These women are saying, "I need to harbor this resentment as a memorial to my hurt because if I don't, no one else will. I can't let him get away with what he did. He should pay somehow and this helps me deal with that." It sounds as if both are saying, "There needs to be a road sign or public address system that declares, 'This person is a wrongdoer.'"

If you follow this methodology, you are overlooking a critical factor. What if God adapted this same outlook? What if God never offered His Son as the ransom to redeem the soul of man back into His good graces? What if God still held a grudge against us for what Adam and Eve allowed to happen in His paradise? The fact is that we would have no hope if Jesus didn't wipe our slate clean. Even if we didn't see the need to apologize, we were still forgiven. So if the very creator of the universe can issue a blanket forgiveness policy, so should we.

JUST THE FACTS

> *OUR LIVES ARE NOT OF ANY USE TO THE LORD NOR IS THE CROSS OF ANY SIGNIFICANCE TO US IF WE DO NOT FIRST FORGIVE EACH OTHER.*

To help put things in their proper perspective I will provide the scriptural texts to support forgiveness. The scripture will serve as the content but how we apply them will serve as the context. Most churches fail to reach the hurting on a consistent basis because leadership forgets the context of the people they are preaching to. Jesus didn't preach, He told stories. He told multi-layered stories (parables) because He knew how people (His children) thought.

These stories were at times simple and at other times more complex. He taught in layers so that people would take the time to dige st His words and their application. Plain white bread won't satisfy your hunger for long, but multi-grain bread takes your stomach more time to digest, thus satisfying your hunger longer. Jesus wanted man to be kept by His word.

Speaking in parables would make humanity slow down and ponder His teaching so that they would internalize and assimilate what was said. If they were able to get up and leave the same way students bolt for the door when it's time for recess, there would be no c hange of mindset or character.

Although we all come from different mindsets relative to forgiveness and varying degrees of hurt; as Christians we can all agree on one thing. We agree that we love the Lord and that we want to show Him this love daily. Jesus is love and wherever you see His name in the bible, it is quite easy to substitute the name Jesus with the word love.

Even in His uncanny ability of maintaining and explaining the Mosaic Laws that He was accused of breaking; He was interpreting them through the eyes of love. That is what He was referring to when He said in (Matthew 5:17), *"Think not that I am come to destroy the law, or the prophets: I am not come to destroy, but to fulfill."*

At the base of Jesus' foundational purpose for coming here are those of forgiveness and love as illustrated in (John 3:16-17) *For God so loved the world that he gave his one and only Son, that whoever believes in him shall not perish but have eternal life. For God did not send his Son into the world to condemn the world, but to save the world through him."*

As Christians we are well aware of the Lord's sacrifice for us but we lose sight of the fact that He was and still is an actual person; a person who expects to be shown love in order to feel loved by us. If this wasn't the case He wouldn't have created Adam for fellowship. Jesus gave plain instructions on how to express our love to Him. In (John 14:16) He says, *"If ye love me, keep my commandments"*

For further clarity in (John 14:23) *Jesus*

answered and said unto him, If a man love me, he will keep my words: and my Father will love him, and we will come unto him, and make our abode with him.

Jesus also said in (2 John 1:6), *"and this is love: that we walk in obedience to his commands. As you have heard from the beginning, his command is that you walk in love."* Jesus goes on to say in (John 15:10), *"If you obey my commands, you will remain in my love, just as I have obeyed my Father's commands and remain in his love.* So we understand that Jesus wants us to be obedient to His commands as a show of our love to Him.

Now let's take a brief look at some of His key commands. In (Luke 10:27) Jesus said, *"Love the Lord your God with all your heart and with all your soul and with all your strength and with all your mind'; and, 'Love your neighbor as yourself.'"*

This scripture explains that if you love God with everything you have then you can love your neighbor as yourself. Then we step up our game of showing God our love a bit more in (MATTHEW 11:25,25) *"Whenever you stand praying, forgive, if you have anything against anyone, so that your Father who is in heaven will also forgive you your transgressions. But if you do not forgive, neither will your Father who is in heaven forgive your transgressions."*

As simple as this scripture is, there are many who completely miss it. Basically Jesus is saying that God cannot engage in any act of forgiving you or hearing your prayer unless you have forgiven first. Remember, Jesus' purpose for hanging on the cross is for the word forgiven.

Now the next scripture is the quintessential example of expectations management from God to us concerning love. If you say you love the Lord and you are having issues with people and how they have treated you then you may want to read the next set of scriptures in bite sized portions. In television this will be called a disclaimer.

(LUKE 6:27-38) "But I say to you who hear: Love your enemies, do good to those who hate you, ^{28} bless those who curse you, and pray for those who spitefully use you. ^{29} To him who strikes you on the one cheek, offer the other also. And from him who takes away your cloak, do not withhold your tunic either. ^{30} Give to everyone who asks of you. And from him who takes away your goods do not ask them back. ^{31} And just as you want men to do to you, you also do to them likewise.

^{32} "But if you love those who love you, what credit is that to you? For even sinners love those who love them. ^{33} And if you do good to those who do good to you, what credit is that to you? For even sinners do the same. ^{34} And if you lend to those

from whom you hope to receive back, what credit is that to you? For even sinners lend to sinners to receive as much back. ^{35} But love your enemies, do good, and lend, hoping for nothing in return; and your reward will be great, and you will be sons of the Most High. For He is kind to the unthankful and evil. ^{36} Therefore be merciful, just as your Father also is merciful.

^{37} "Judge not, and you shall not be judged. Condemn not, and you shall not be condemned. Forgive, and you will be forgiven. ^{38} Give, and it will be given to you: good measure, pressed down, shaken together, and running over will be put into your bosom. For with the same measure that you use, it will be measured back to you."

Jesus' commands are basically these:
- **6. Love your enemies.**
- **7. Do good to those who hate you.**
- **8. Bless those who curse you.**
- **9. Pray for those who mistreat you.**
- **10. Do not retaliate (v. 29a).**
- **11. Give freely (vv. 29b-30).**
- **12. Treat others the way you want to be treated (v. 31). This kind of love marks one off as distinctive (vv. 32-34), and as having the same characteristics as the heavenly Father (v. 35).**

I told you this wouldn't be easy to read if you're not there yet. To be honest my friend, most of us are not here yet either. This is why the Church is in the same spot that Jesus left it in almost 2 millennia ago. The fact remains that we need to get here if we want to see Him. (James 4:17) *"Therefore to him that knoweth to do good, and doeth [it] not, to him it is sin."* Simply put, many of us are not just guilty of the commission of sin; we are also guilty of the sin of omission.

LET HE WHO IS WITHOUT SIN…

Jesus had a way of allowing humans the grace to actually think that they could consider themselves on His level, when He could have snatched the breath from their lungs with a subtle wave of His hand. But instead of judgment for man's arrogance, He showed patient love. This is illustrated in (John 8:1-12): *"But Jesus went to the Mount of Olives. At dawn he appeared again in the temple courts; where all the people gathered around him, and he sat down to teach them. The teachers of the law and the Pharisees brought in a woman caught in adultery. They made her stand before the group and said to Jesus, 'Teacher, this woman was caught in the act of adultery.*

In the Law Moses commanded us to stone such women. Now what do you say?' They were using this question as a trap, in order to have a basis for accusing him. But Jesus bent down and started to write on the ground with his finger. When they kept on questioning him, he straightened up and said to them, 'If any one of you is without sin, let him be the first to throw a stone at her.' Again he stooped down and wrote on the ground. At this, those who heard began to go away one at a time, the older ones first, until only Jesus was left, with the woman still standing there. Jesus straightened up and asked her, 'Woman, where are they? Has no one condemned you?' 'No one, sir,' she said. 'Then neither do I condemn you,' Jesus declared. 'Go now and leave your life of sin.'"

Notice how calm Jesus was in the midst of what would a perilous situation for most people. Under Israeli law in those days, adultery constituted a heinous, vile thing. For a woman to be caught in that sin, there would be a call for her public stoning. Yet Jesus told her that even the Son of God would forgive her as long as she agreed to willingly stop sinning.

Most of us are all too willing to hang others on the cross for their wrongs. Instead of acknowledging that we all have feet made of clay, too many of us are eager to join the lynch mob and watch people literally get choked to death by the words we use to strangle them.

Let's take a look at the Ten Commandments from Exodus 20:3-17 to see if we can pass the red-faced test.

One: "You shall have no other gods before me."

Many of us fail in this command the moment we identify ourselves by what we do as a profession and what we aspire to achieve. In this economy, many of us are more concerned about paying our bills than our daily walk with God.

Two: "You shall not make for yourself an idol in the form of anything in heaven above or on the earth beneath or in the waters below."

This commandment means that we should not create in our minds what we do not know for certain about God. Today's modernism has given man the audacity to bring God's reasoning down to His level. This contradicts the words of Moses: *"The secret things belong to the Lord our God, but the things revealed belong to us and to our children forever, that we may follow all the words of this law."* (Deuteronomy 29:29).

Three: "You shall not misuse the name of the Lord your God, for the Lord will not hold anyone guiltless who misuses his name."

You likely hear His name misused a dozen times a day. People often exclaim, "Oh my G---" or even worse, damn others in anger while using God's name. In the Old Testament, God's name was considered so holy it could not be uttered.

Four: "Remember the Sabbath day by keeping it holy."

The Sabbath was intended to be a day of rest and worship, not a day to catch up with everything at the office, go shopping, or watch sports all day.

Five: "Honor your father and your mother, so that you may live long in the land the Lord your God is giving you."

This is the first commandment that comes with a promise. Paul amplified on this in his letter to the Ephesians: *"Children, obey your parents in the Lord, for this is right. 'Honor your father and mother'—which is the first commandment with a promise—'so that it may go well with you and that you may enjoy long life on the earth.'"* (Ephesians 6:1-3).

Yet how many people (including Christians) dishonor their parents, whether by their words, their actions, or simply their neglect of aging parents? We can tell our ability to keep this commandment by the words and thoughts we have toward our parents if we are still blessed to have them with us.

Six: "You shall not murder."

As simple and straight forward as this commandment is, how many times have we thought murderous thoughts toward our enemies, or and even loved ones? How many times have we spoken words maliciously that killed someone's spirit? Yet, 1 John 3:15 says, *"Anyone who hates a brother or sister is a murderer, and you know that no murderer has eternal life residing in him."*

Seven: "You shall not commit adultery."

If you dwell on an attraction to someone else outside your marriage then you have already committed adultery in your mind. As Jesus said in the Sermon on the Mount, *"You have heard that it was said, 'You shall not commit adultery.' But I tell you that anyone who looks at a woman lustfully has already committed adultery with her in his heart."* (Matthew 5:27-28). Most of us don't follow our thoughts and fantasies for fear of being caught, not because it's wrong.

Eight: "You shall not steal."

We won't even go there. Just be honest with yourself and don't try to insult the mind of God. Don't kid yourself: taking home a box of paper clips or nice pens from work, or grabbing extra napkins or other supplies at a restaurant, is still theft.

Nine: "You shall not give false testimony against your neighbor."

Another no-brainer: If you have ever lied or gossiped about a co-worker, a neighbor, or even a member of your family—without any idea of whether the stories you're passing along are true—and still participate in such tale-bearing, God considers this bearing false witness.

Ten: "You shall not covet your neighbor's house. You shall not covet your neighbor's wife, or his manservant or maidservant, his ox or donkey, or anything that belongs to your neighbor."

My comment here is similar to that just mentioned above. If you envy anyone's lifestyle, good fortune, or God's favor, this is called covetousness.

OBEDIENCE

When you think about it in God's eyes, few of us obey the Ten Commandments as He intended them to be honored. What does that say about us? Christ's words from Matthew 7:5 come to mind: *"You hypocrite, first take the plank out of your own eye, and then you will see clearly to remove the speck from your brother's eye."* This is why Paul wrote that *"all have sinned and fall short of the glory of God."* (Romans 3:23).

God knew the nature of man is to lie; cheat, steal, hide and finger point before he would accept blame or turn the fault toward him. As soon as God asked Adam about the sin he committed, Adam passed the blame to Eve instead of taking responsibility for the fact that he was in charge.

Likewise, we often look to complain, play the "blame game" or assume victim status before we look within to originate change. We all are familiar with the subtle changes we need to make within ourselves, especially when the world around us is not willing to do so. Many psychologists advise that if your circumstances are not going to change, then you should change the way you look at those circumstances.

We will soon find that less energy is required to simply have a change of mind and heart so that we can move on with our lives instead of deciding to remain stuck in our ways. At the end of the day you will feel a burden lifted.

> *The Lord will get the glory and the enemy will be stuck with the story.*

Now that I have covered what the Bible says about forgiveness, how do we let go of the grudge and practically apply the premise of forgiveness to our lives? Here are some pointers:

1. Understand that if you are a Christian, forgiveness is something you must offer in order to make it to heaven. It is easier to make it to heaven hooked on crack, alcohol, or pornography than to choose not to forgive

someone. Remember what God has forgiven you of and the story of the thief on the cross.

2. By holding on to a grudge you give control of your life to Satan and the offender. That is like drinking poison and expecting the other person to die. You replay the offense over and over in your mind like a scratched CD, rehearsing the offense and carrying bitterness and negativity into every relationship. Not to mention that doing so means you are out of fellowship with God.

3. Making the decision to forgive is like coming to a state of repentance. You must decide to make a role change, turning away from the role of victim. You must tell yourself that the person who hurt you also needs God the same way that you do. Ask the Holy Spirit to reveal the shortcomings in their life. Remember on the cross that Jesus told His Father, "Forgive them, for they know not what they do."

4. Understand that true forgiveness does not necessarily bring an apology. Nor does it mean that the other person will change. Sometimes he or she is deceased or otherwise not reachable.

> *At its root, forgiveness is between you and God. Like repentance, it is not a single act, but a mindset and lifestyle change.*

5. Simply forgetting is not forgiveness. Forgetting is denial. That which is hidden comes into sight at the most inopportune times. Just because an offense is hidden doesn't mean God can't see it. The eyes of the Lord are every place, beholding the good and evil in the heart of men and women.

6. Don't seek revenge or sit waiting for God to strike the offender dead. Your role is to forgive. That is your purpose. Stay in your lane. God has more resources and bandwidth to punish than you do. As you take these steps, remember these scriptures: *"Do not take revenge, my friends, but leave room for God's wrath, for it is written: 'It is mine to avenge; I will repay,' says the Lord."* (Romans 12:19-AKJV); *"Do not rejoice when your enemy falls, and do not let your heart be glad when he stumbles."* (Proverbs 24:17).

7. *Salvation is the roof we live under that Jesus provided. It shields us from the hellfire and brimstone until He returns to claim us. Forgiveness is the rent we pay to live under that protection.*

8. Forgiveness is not about humans, but the

audience of one that you have with Jesus through the Holy Spirit. It is truly only the Spirit of God that can bring forgiveness for sin. We need the Holy Ghost in order to forgive.

9. If you are the offender in a particular situation, apologize. Own up to what you did and ask for the other person's forgiveness. You may not receive it right away. That is up to the Lord and them to work through. Just know that you did what you were supposed to do.

10. According to numerous clinical studies, forgiveness has a variety of physiological benefits. Among them are healthier relationships, greater spiritual and psychological well-being, less stress and hostility, lower blood pressure, fewer symptoms of depression, anxiety and chronic pain, and lower risk of alcohol and substance abuse.

11. I know people who hold on to resentment like an old smelly coat. As soon as the right season comes, they reach into the closet and put it on. Instantly they become transformed into a vintage movie projector and relive all the wrong done to them, as if they are relating it for the first time. Slowly people start to tune them out or even leave the room. Forgiving makes you more pleasant to be around.

12. Remember that when you forgive, you become a vessel that the Lord can use for His purposes. When He searches for a willing vessel, He will look into the glass and see His reflection, not the old, dirty residue of unforgiveness.

THE HARDEST THING TO DO

About two years ago I was asked to serve as a pallbearer for a funeral at our church for a twenty-something year old man who got shot and killed. I am not o ne to pry into others' lives unless I am asked to c ounsel them and it is necessary. So I did not find out any details; I just knew that he was the son of a Latino family who had just joined the church. One Sunday before services I was making copies of a schedule for one of my classes when I saw the victim's mother.

Her name is Lizette. She is beautiful and has a transparent spirit— the kind of person who walks into a room and you want to know more about her. She volunteers with the children's nursery and helps in any way possible. She was speaking with another member and was explaining that the trial for her son's murderer had just taken place, and that she had peace about it and had forgiven his killer.

Since I didn't know the details at this point, there was no way that I could play dumb. I told

Lizette that I never knew what happened or if the shooter got caught. She replied that his killer was his girlfriend. At her trial, the jury found her innocent and she walked.

My stomach fell to my shoes as I looked into her eyes and heard the story for the first time. With incredible poise and strength, this mother had been dealing with this in stages. As she reflected peace that could only come from the work of the Holy Spirit, I saw God's handiwork.

Lizette told me that she felt her testimony would one day bless someone else. One of my next classes was on the subject of forgiveness. I asked her if she would be a guest speaker. That day, I taught on forgiveness (much as how you've read in this chapter) and introduced Lizette.

She told of how after her son's girlfriend shot him, she went through the full gamut of emotions. Yet the Spirit of God summoned her to simply let go of this anger and resentment. *So, she told the girl that she forgave her and simply moved on.* How powerful!

There is nothing more unnatural in this world than for a parent to have to bury their child. I can think of no greater pain for anyone to bear. Here stood this woman, speaking of this pain and how she allowed God to completely take this burden from her, including working through her loving family and church family. Although she never had the opportunity to say, "I love you" or to hug her son one last time, she said that she knew that forgiveness was God's way and that we were first forgiven without offering an apology.

Lizette said she hopes that her son suddenly being taken from this earth can serve as a testimony to other young people and parents on how to love their families: *"Tomorrow is not promised to anyone, which is why you must live responsibly and lovingly."* As Lizette stood before this group, I saw God's glory surround her. I knew that this would be the launch of another incredible chapter in her life. There was not a dry eye in the room as she finished speaking; she received the love and respect that a woman of her stature deserved.

I have covered a lot of material in this chapter and know most of it you likely already knew. However, I hope that the information has been packaged in a way that you can readily use it and apply it to your life or pass it along to someone else who needs to hear it. I'm not a salesperson for forgiveness. Nor I am trying to convince you of something that I get a bonus for accomplishing. I am simply saying that forgiveness is not an outfit you choose to wear one day and shed the next. It is a privilege offered us by our Lord and Savior, Jesus Christ. Choosing to accept this forgiveness and pass it along is His commandment, one we will follow if we love Him.

Choosing not to forgive is telling Him that what we have endured is greater than what He endured, so we are denying His suffering and the cross. If so, we are choosing to live beneath our privilege. My prayer for you is that you choose to do this in the name of love for Jesus and no one else. I pray that before you close your eyes tonight that you choose to let go of this worthless token known as the burdensome past and that you give it to the Lord, who has been patiently waiting to take it from you.

Whenever you were offended, Jesus knew thatwhen it happened there would come a day that you would read these words and that you would feel the peace and consolation of your heavenly Father's voice in the bosom of your soul. Jesus wants to take the pain from you. He wants you to know that you deserve to live free of this, regardless of what you've been made to feel. So many have died and left this earth carrying burdens to their grave without feeling God's pain-relieving and burden-lifting power. Jesus doesn't want you to be one of them.

I offer this prayer for you:

Father God, in the name of Jesus, I give my beloved friend over to you to heal and cleanse the burden in their heart. Completely lift their hurt and pain from them. Lord Jesus, come into their heart and do the house cleaning in their soul that only You are qualified to accomplish. Show them Your power to lift the invisible stains from their heart. Replace the hole and damage with the promise of joy and life eternal. Let there be no further personal torment and persecution, but complete relief and the ability to breathe deeply. Let my beloved friend be able to have the best night's rest ever as he or she rests in Your personal approval and assurance of better days ahead. They do this now in obedience, surrender, and the hope in You and You alone. In Jesus' mighty name, Amen!

My brother, my sister, my friend, I pray that you repeated that prayer knowing that the Lord meant it for you. I wrote this book with the express purpose of you being of improved service to God and more complete for your personal fulfillment and the lives you love and touch.

Please read this chapter again and again until the words and scriptures within are no longer just ink on a page but actual cues that speak to your existence and state of mind. The scriptures are the living Word. They must take life before you can move on just as they did with Lizette. You can do this!

For your ease and convenience, below I have included numerous scriptures on forgiveness. Please read them daily until your past becomes your testimony of healing. This testimony will be for you to share with the person God will send your way who is also living beneath their privilege and in need of some truth.

SCRIPTURES ON FORGIVENESS

Matthew 5:9-12:"Blessed are the peacemakers, for they will be called sons of God. Blessed are those who are persecuted because of righteousness, for theirs is the kingdom of heaven. Blessed are you when people insult you, persecute you and falsely say all kinds of evil against you because of me. Rejoice and be glad, because great is your reward in heaven, for in the same way they persecuted the prophets who were before you."

Matthew 5:44: "But I tell you: Love your enemies and pray for those who persecute you."

Matthew 6:12: "Forgive us our debts, as we also have forgiven our debtors."

Matthew 6:14-15: "For if you forgive men when they sin against you, your heavenly Father will also forgive you. But if you do not forgive men their sins, your Father will not forgive your sins."

Matthew 7:2-5: "For in the same way you judge others, you will bejudged, and with the measure you use, it will be measured to you. Why do you look at the speck of sawdust in your brother's eye and pay no attention to the plank in your own eye? How can you say to your brother, 'Let me take the speck out of your eye,' when all the time there is a plank in your own eye? You hypocrite, first take the plank out of your own eye, and then you will see clearly to remove the speck from your brother's eye."

Matthew 18:21-35: "Then Peter came to Jesus and asked, 'Lord, how many times shall I forgive my brother when he sins against me? Up to seven times?' Jesus answered, 'I tell you, not seven times, but seventy-seven times.' "Therefore, the kingdom of heaven is like a king who wanted to settle accounts with his servants. As he began the settlement, a man who owed him ten thousand talents was brought to him. Since he was not able to pay, the master ordered that he and his wife and his children and all that he had be sold to repay the debt."

"The servant fell on his knees before him. 'Be

patient with me,' he begged, 'and I will pay back everything.' The servant's master took pity on him, canceled the debt and let him go."

"But when that servant went out, he found one of his fellow servants who owed him a hundred denarii. He grabbed him and began to choke him. 'Pay back what you owe me!' he demanded. His fellow servant fell to his knees and begged him, 'Be patient with me, and I will pay you back.' But he refused. Instead, he went off and had the man thrown into prison until he could pay the debt."

"When the other servants saw what had happened, they were greatly distressed and went and told their master everything that had happened. Then the master called the servant in. 'You wicked servant,' he said, 'I canceled all that debt of yours because you begged me to. Shouldn't you have had mercy on your fellow servant just as I had on you?'

"In anger his master turned him over to the jailers to be tortured, until he should pay back all he owed. This is how my heavenly Father will treat each of you unless you forgive your brother from your heart."

Mark 11:25-26: "Whenever you stand praying, forgive, if you have anything against anyone, so that your Father who is in heaven will also forgive you your transgressions. But if you do not forgive, neither will your Father who is in heaven forgive your transgressions."

Luke 6:35-37: "But love your enemies, do good to them, and lend to them without expecting to get anything back. Then your reward will be great, and you will be sons of the Most High, because he is kind to the ungrateful and wicked. Be merciful, just as your Father is merciful. Do not judge, and you will not be judged. Do not condemn, and you will not be condemned. Forgive, and you will be forgiven."

Luke 11:4: "Forgive us our sins, for we also forgive everyone who sins against us. And lead us not into temptation."

Luke 15:27-30: "'Your brother has come,' he replied, 'and your father has killed the fattened calf because he has him back safe and sound.' The older brother became angry and refused to go in. So his father went out and pleaded with him. But he answered his father, 'Look! All these years I've been slaving for you and never disobeyed your orders. Yet you never gave me even a young goat so I could celebrate with my friends. But when this son of yours who has squandered your property with prostitutes comes home, you kill the fattened calf for him!'"

Luke 17:3- 4: "So watch yourselves. If your brother sins, rebuke him, and if he repents, forgive him. If he sins against you seven times in a day, and seven times comes back to you and says, 'I repent,' forgive him."

Luke 23:34: "Jesus said, 'Father, forgive them, for they do n ot know what they are doing.' And they divided up his clothes by casting lots."

Romans 5:8: "But God demonstrates his own love for us in this: While we were still sinners, Christ died for us."

Romans 12:9-10: "Love must be sincere. Hate what is evil; cling to what is good. Be devoted to one another in brotherly love. Honor one another above yourselves."

Romans 12:16: "Live in harmony with one another. Do not be proud, but be willing to associate with people of low position. Do not be conceited."

Romans 12:19-21: "Do not take revenge, my friends, but leave room for God's wrath, for it is written: 'It is mine to avenge; I will repay,' says the Lord. On the contrary: 'If your enemy is hungry, feed him; if he is thirsty, give him something to drink. In doing this, you will heap burning coals on his head.' Do not be overcome by evil, but overcome evil with good." (emphasis added).

Romans 14:1: "Accept him whose faith is weak, without passing judgment on disputable matters."

Romans 15:1-2: "We who are strong ought to bear with the failings of the weak and not to please ourselves. Each of us should please his neighbor for his good, to build him up."

1 Corinthians 2:12 -15: "We have not received the spirit of the world but the Spirit who is from God, that we may understand what God has freely given us. This is what we speak, not in words taught us by human wisdom but in words taught by the Spirit, expressing spiritual truths in spiritual words. The man without the Spirit does not accept the things that come from the Spirit of God, for they are foolishness to him, and he cannot understand them, because they are spiritually discerned. The spiritual man makes judgments about all things, but he himself is not subject to any man's judgment."

1 Corinthians 3:1-3: "Brothers, I could not address you as spiritual but as worldly--mere infants in Christ. I gave you milk, not solid food, for you were not yet ready for it. Indeed, you are

still not ready. You are still worldly. For since there is jealousy and quarreling among you, are you not w orldly? Are you not acting like mere men?"

1 Corinthians 6:7: "The very fact that you have lawsuits among you means you have been completely defeated already. Why not r ather be wronged? Why not rather be cheated?"

1 Corinthians 13:4-8: "Love is p atient, love is kind. It does not envy, it does not boast, it is not proud. It is not rude, it is not self-seeking, it is not easily angered, it keeps no record of wrongs.
Love does not delight in evil but rejoices with the truth. It always protects, always trusts, always hopes, always perseveres. Love never fails. But where there are prophecies, they will cease;
where there are tongues, they will be stilled; where there is knowledge, it will pass away."

1 Corinthians 14:20: "Brothers, stop thinking like children. In regard to evil be infants, but in your thinking be adults."

2 Corinthians 2:6-7: "The punishment inflicted on him by the majority is sufficient for him. Now instead, you ought to forgive and comfort him, so that he will not be overwhelmed by excessive sorrow."

Galatians 6:1-2: "Brothers, if someone is caught in a sin, you who are spiritual should restore him gently. But watch yourself, or you also may be tempted. Carry each other's burdens, and in this way you will fulfill the law of Christ."

Ephesians 4:1-3: "As a prisoner for the Lord, then, I urge you to live a life worthy of the calling you have received. Be completely humble and gentle; be patient, bearing with one another in love. Make every effort to keep the unity of the Spirit through the bond of peace."

Ephesians 4:32: "Be kind and compassionate to one another, forgiving each other, just as in Christ God forgave you."

Philippians 2:3-4: "Do nothing out of selfish ambition or vain conceit, but in humility consider others better than yourselves. Each of you should look not only to your own interests, but also to the interests of others."

Philippians 3:15: "All of us who are mature should take such a view of things. And if on some point you think differently, that too God will make clear to you."

Colossians 3:12-13: "Therefore, as God's chosen people, holy and dearly loved, clothe yourselves with compassion, kindness, humility, gentleness and patience. Bear with each other and forgive whatever grievances you may have against one another. Forgive as the Lord forgave you."

2 Timothy 2:24- 26: "And the Lord's servant must not quarrel; instead, he must be kind to everyone, able to teach, not resentful. Those who op pose him he must gently instruct, in the hope that God will grant them repentance leading them to a knowledge of the truth, and that they will come to their senses and escape from the trap of the devil, who has taken them captive to do his will."

James 1:5: "If any of you lacks wisdom, he should ask God, who gives generously to a ll without finding fault, and it will be given to him."

James 1:12: "Blessed is the man who perseveres under trial, because when he has stood the test, he will receive the crown of life that God has promised to those who love him."

James 2:12-13: "Speak and act as those who are going to be judged by the law that gives freedom, because judgment without mercy will be shown to anyone who has not been merciful. Mercy triumphs over judgment!"

James 3:13-18: "Who is wise and understanding among you? Let him show it by his good life, by deeds done in the humility that comes from wisdom. But if you harbor bitter envy and selfish ambition in your hearts, do not boast about it or deny the truth. Such 'wisdom' does not come down from heaven but is earthly, unspiritual, of the devil. For where you have envy and selfish ambition, there you find disorder and every evil practice. But the wisdom that comes from heaven is first of all pure; then peace-loving, considerate, submissive, full of mercy and good fruit, impartial and sincere. Peacemakers who sow in peace raise a harvest of righteousness."

James 5:19-20: "My brothers, if one of you should wander from the truth and someone should bring him back, remember this: Whoever turns a sinner from the error of his way will save him from death and cover over a multitude of sins."

1 Peter 2:17: "Show proper respect to everyone: Love the brotherhood of believers, fear God, honor the king."

1 Peter 2:21-23: "To this you were called, because Christ suffered for you, leaving you an example that you should follow in his steps. He committed no sin, and no deceit was found in his mouth. When they hurled their insults at him, he did not retaliate; when he suffered, he made no threats. Instead, he entrusted himself to him who judges justly."

1 Peter 3:8-9: "Finally, all of you, live in harmony with one another; be sympathetic, love as brothers,

be compassionate and humble. Do not repay evil with evil or insult with insult, but with blessing, because to this you were called so that you may inherit a blessing."

1 Peter 4:8: "Above all, love each other deeply, because love covers over a multitude of sins."

1 John 1:9: "If we confess our sins, he is faithful and just and will forgive us our sins and purify us from all unrighteousness."

1 John 3:15: "Anyone who hates his brother is a murderer, and you know that no murderer has eternal life in him."

1 John 3:18: "Dear children, let us not love with words or tongue but with actions and in truth."

Jude 1:19: "These are the men who divide you, who follow mere natural instincts and do not have the Spirit."

CHAPTER FIVE
ME TIME

THE QUALITY TIME YOU SPEND WITH YOURSELF WILL REVEAL THAT PURPOSE IS NOT A DESTINATION BUT SEIZING THE OPPORTUNITIES THAT PRESENT THEMSELVES ALONG LIFE'S JOURNEY.

WHAT IS ME TIME?

Whether you call it "me time," "time for self," "alone time," "time out" or "pampering time," these phrases are known the world over to mean the same thing: getting away. It doesn't matter to where or for how long. What does matter is that you do. When you have had a life filled with drama, obligations or just simple neglect, the laws of balance and self-preservation dictate that you take some time to calibrate your mind, body and soul to the precise settings ordained by the Master. *Me Time* simply says, "I need to get some sleep, eat a healthy meal, drink some water, cleanse my thoughts and retune my spirit through intense prayer and study of the Word." If your time and resources are adequate, *Me Time* may involve some solitary time away from your routine and pampering your senses with sumptuous sights, sounds, tastes and wholesome pleasures.

People, especially those who are used to continually giving of themselves, can get so accustomed to maintaining and keeping up with everyone else's needs that they forget about *taking care of themselves*. When this happens, people place so much emphasis on everyone else's welfare that they overlook their own. The best insurance policy for your loved ones is being there. If you can't remember the last time you had physical and some blood work done, it's been too long.

If you can't remember the last time you had a pelvic exam or a mammography, then it has been too long. If you have never sought counseling for obvious emotional and physical symptoms that you have been keeping a secret, please—for the sake of those who love you the most and will miss you the most—take some *Me Time* and get yourself checked out before it's too late. Now that you have overcome your past, it's time to start living for your future. *Me Time* is a celebration of you.

Pursue this celebration with the same passion and determination as the women with the issue of blood found in the Gospels. She had a menstrual cycle that came and stayed with her for 12 years. She was determined despite what the circumstances of the crowd dictated. She wasn't going to let the crowd keep her from **her time** to heal. So she got down on her belly and crawled toward her objective which was the only part of Jesus that she felt worthy of and able to touch; His hem. Her determination to withstand certain criticism and persecution for even thinking herself worthy brought her back a change for the rest of her life. Dear woman, press for this time for your change and discovery.

REHEARSAL HAS BEEN CANCELED

When it comes to moving forward, one of the biggest struggles you will face is getting closure with the parts of life that brought you pain. ***Closure is the verb that makes forgiveness a reality. Closure brings the inner peace of knowing that you will not rehearse this in your mind any longer.***

Do you remember when your favorite song played on the radio constantly and everyone would either sing or hum it like a secret we all shared? After several months or years that melody is not as popular; it is no longer in style. At some point that song became old and outdated. Whenever you found yourself singing that song out loud, some people would look at you strangely because you were singing a song that didn't fit anymore. That's how holding on to things without closure appears. Everyone has moved on but you are still rehearsing that same old song.

During your **Me Time** celebration you must decide that forgiveness was enough and that your spirit is too vital a commodity to allow just any noise to vibrate within your sacred corridors. This is the same spirit that gives you communion with God and your destiny. In order to achieve the closure you deserve, you must first decide that what Jesus gave on the cross was simply enough to cancel rehearsal.

SOME ASSEMBLY REQUIRED

This phrase can cause extreme anxiety if you lack an engineer's patience and critical thinking skills. *Some assembly required* speaks of the ability to follow detailed instructions and having the character to withstand the objective criticism that can come from an obvious inability to deliver.

Here is where you must ask yourself such serious questions as: Am I bringing the same negative, destructive patterns into every situation? Am I always the victim or sometimes the offender who rejects accountability and improvement? Perhaps your ego has overstepped God's grace and the rest of the world is now seeing the truth. Have you become so steeped in instant gratification that you have lost all grasp of discipline? Finally, are you stuck at the same point as last year because of fear?

The **_Me Time_** celebration is when you learn how to apply the principles of truth to your life. Remember that in chapter 3, "Taking Dominon," we addressed such principles of truth as:
- *Truth merits no reward, nor does it dignify a response; truth is supreme and therefore absolute.*
- *When we internalize this reality, then changing one's self and accepting the world as it is around us becomes easier.*

During this celebration, don't be fearful of embracing your frailties and strengths. Only when you become intimate with something can you effect change. In some cases it may come as a surprise that you have been the cause of some of the failed relationships in your life. In a deeper analysis, it may occur to you that you have attracted the abusive people who brought down the behaviors that you had to endure.

Me Time is where you may embrace the fact that you have never been able to lean on anyone because you have always been the strongest person you know. Shedding a sense of false strength is where you can capture intimacy with God. This is because you remove all false idols that separate you from God, including that sense of self-sufficiency. The Lord is the only knight in shining armor that gets credit for bailing you out and putting your pieces back together.

As you sit a nd contemplate the intricate components that make you a beautiful, captivating person, try to see the presence you embody. Look at yourself in the mirror; see yourself as the world sees you. Smile. Practice smiling until you actually like what you see. Put on your favorite stand-up comedian (or comedienne) and observe your reactions in the mirror to what they are saying.

I'm not suggesting engaging in vanity. I am merely saying to become familiar with the person who has been neglected for so long. This is the best way to give yourself an embrace from within. Approve of yourself by admiring your smile, skin tone and physique.

Tell yourself when you get out of the shower that you smell good. If you live alone, talk to yourself, audibly, in encouraging terms. Get to know the sound of your voice as you speak kind things to yourself. Take heart in and appreciate the fact that you can wash and dress yourself—
millions of people on this planet must depend on others to do that for them.

As you dress, take the time to enjoy the way

you wear your femininity or masculinity. Do you know that there are millions of people today who you think are beautiful (or handsome) but have never been told that they are attractive by their fathers or another patriarch in their family?

When was the last time you treated yourself to a facial, a day spa or a manicure or a pedicure…just because? When was the last time you took yourself out to dinner and enjoyed an evening out by yourself, just for yourself? This celebration of *Me Time* needs to be seen as a real celebration for someone real and special, because you are real and special. Jesus didn't die for the rest of the world and not you. He died for His relationship with you. Matthew 18:12 says,
"What do you think? If a man owns a hundred sheep, and one of them wanders away, will he not leave the ninety-nine on the hills and go to look for the one that wandered off?"

The wonderful thing about Jesus and God being different manifestations of the same Spirit is they can pursue the needs of one and not deplete their existence for the other.

Jesus can pursue you in every area you want Him to oc cupy and still be there for the other people for whom you are praying. Take care in analyzing yourself during this time and don't get too critical or too lenient. The objective is to get to the point where you know yourself better than the people around you.

With this knowledge of yourself, create a list of your strengths and weaknesses. Then review the list to see which column has the most checkmarks. Next, see how your weaknesses compare to your strengths. For instance, you don't want to be a great critical thinker but poor at taking correction or offering accountability. You also don't want to be a great listener but unable to express your feelings if your life depended on it.

Take this assessment seriously; this may be the best gift you can give yourself (other than accepting Christ into your heart). You don't have to share this list with anyone unless you choose to, but be brutally honest.

Look to the perfect Manufacturer to address your defects, not another person. Through the blood of Jesus, God still sees you as perfect.

Unlike man, *Christ's love doesn't judge your faults. Nor do they compete with your strengths.* They simply convict and convince His children of the perfection of His love. All He cares about is that each of His followers love Him with all their heart and treat each other with the good sense, the way each person expect Him to treat them. That's all. It is that simple.

WHO AM I?

Always take stock of your inherent value, not what you do for a living or the socio-economic status you have achieved. If you are a businessperson and I asked about your identity, don't respond that you are an accountant or a general manager. If you are a lawyer or a doctor, you still shouldn't align your identity with how you earn a living. Human status does not impress God. He is the one who can measure the metrics of the universe in the palm of His hand, so therefore what you have amassed via the opportunities He has afforded you is of little or no significance to Him.

What pleases God is your ability to follow His commandments, as I reviewed in "Taking Dominion." God wants to fellowship with individuals who love Him enough to seek His face and want to turn from their wicked ways. God wants people who are willing to love unconditionally and give without any need to get back. If you will give as though you are giving to God, forgive as though He caused the offense and loves as though it were the only emotion He had programmed into you, and then you can truly say that you know who you are. You wi ll be inextricably intertwined with the Spirit who created all spirits.

As you seek definition in your personhood, ask

the Lord to complete you in all the areas where you are lacking. No matter what our age, we are all similar to children who roam the school yard looking for someone to play with, except we are more sophisticated in hiding our feelings and insecurities. Open your heart to the Lord and ask Him to complete you. When I say complete you, I mean that only He can fill all the empty spaces that you are trying so vigorously to fill.

Everyone has some kind of generational curse that seemingly defined them as a child. For some it was selfishness or cold-hearted behavior inherited from a grandparent or parent. These traits have defined many people for most of their lives. When they realize that these qualities have not brought success, they are forced to place these outward manifestations behind lock and chain. But what can you do to satisfy the innate urge and to console the hurt of knowing you have not been the best person?

When you first awake, try this before you have a conversation with anyone else:

1. Find a quiet place and say the Holy Spirit Morning Greeting in the "Taking Dominion" chapter.

2. After completing that prayer, ask the Holy Spirit for His guidance and instruction through

all the dark places of your life. Tell Him that you desperately need Him to even out the wrinkles in your character.

3. Ask the Lord to eliminate every generational curse that's been handed down to you.

4. Ask the Holy Spirit to give you the courage and wisdom to accept the changes that you must make in your life in order to accommodate His will.

5. Cry out to God the same way you would if your legs were bound and you were thrown into a 12-foot-deep pool of ice-cold water. Your desperate cries for life-saving help would penetrate the heavenly atmosphere and touch the heart of Jesus to summon every angel and worldly asset to come to your rescue.

6. The same is true in your current state of dealing with issues that are killing you slowly and separating you from God's love. There is

7. Ask the Lord to open your eyes to the people and the situations in your life that are taking away from your destiny rather than contributing to it.

8. Ask the Lord to eliminate the multiple choices so that you will only walk the path that He has given you. For so long you have been

distracted by others and their agenda. Now, isn't it time that you pursue what God has for you?

9. God is a God of completion. You can even ask the Lord to discipline your mind and cravings so you can eat less unhealthy foods and desire more of the good foods. When it comes to food, our God is also a God of portion control. If you put Him in a box like the rest of society, then He will only do small things in your life. If you see Him as the God of the universe you will see Him perform great and mighty works through you.

10. Literally place a list of bad habits on a table in front of you, such as the computer that has you addicted to secret sins, social networking sites, or food items. Form a covenant with the Lord for each one by asking Him to remove carnal desires in this area and in return you will give Him an even cleaner vessel to use for His glory. It has worked for me and scores of other men and women.

HERE IS HOW

Pray this prayer:

Father God, in the name of Jesus I am in desperate need of You filling every area of my

life. Lord, I know that I have not been living the way that You intended. I am sorry for whatever I have allowed to come between us. I know that I am not totally to blame but I am not totally innocent, either. Father, please forgive me for anything that I have done that has grieved your Spirit and caused You to turn from me. Lord, this very moment I re-commit my life and all that I am and ever will be to Your service. Lord, you are my Savior. I ask that you completely come into my life through your Holy Spirit.

Lord Jesus, there are things in my life that I have inherited. There are also things that I have created as false idols and vain imaginations. Please rebuke the spirit and intent of those characteristics and remove them from my spirit. Please remove the taste for those desires forever. Lord, replace those bad habits, secret sins and fleshly and sinful pleasures with the desire I have for You at this moment. Teach me to study your Word and to pray and commune with You throughout my day with the same drive I once used to pursue sinful ways.

Holy Spirit, guide me to the choices that bring You glory and praise. Teach and guide me by eliminating distractions and multiple choices that situations may bring into my life. Lord, I cannot serve two masters. I know that

You are the only Master of my life. Please give me a new identity in You. I will be careful to give You all the glory and praise. In Jesus' name, Amen!

If you have sincerely said this prayer, you have allowed the very hand of God to clear the atmosphere of false filters and demonic attacks on your life. Every demon and hell hound has been sent running. Now it is up to you to stay the course in order to keep them away.

KNOWLEDGE IS POWER

Never underestimate the power of knowledge. Take your *Me Time* as an opportunity to read and learn about things that are outside your comfort zone. For instance, if you have no interest in politics or sports, remember that it won't hurt to know the answer to such questions as: What NFL quarterback threw the most touchdown passes in history? Or, who is the longest serving U.S. Supreme Court justice? Do you see how something you are not interested in can suddenly become interesting? Did you want to know the answers to those two pieces of trivia? The answer is, you have to look it up for yourself. Besides, if I gave you the answer, you would miss out on the fun of finding out on your own.

Those two questions are just a small sample of the kinds of tidbits of information you can glean from reading and research. Adding knowledge to your repertoire makes you a more interesting person. Becoming an informed individual sends your personal and social "stock value" through the roof. No one likes a know-it-all, but everyone likes people who have relevant and entertaining insights or observations about current issues.

BE THE THERMOSTAT NOT THE THERMOMETER

It's amazing how two things can be so close in relation yet so different in purpose. A thermostat is the device on the wall that turns the heating and cooling on for a room to accommodate your pre-set desired temperature. The thermostat tells the cooling and heating elements when to function and for how long. The thermostat controls the atmosphere in a room.

A thermometer basically gives the reading of the temperature. Its job is to simply react to what the thermostat creates. You must decide which of these devices you have become. Are you the person who responds to the atmosphere created by others, or are you the one who creates the atmosphere. When you walk into a room do others pause and take note of your manifestation and the mere presence you've brought by simply being there? Or do they not even notice that you exist. If your answer is the latter, then it's time to

> **Be the change you wish to see in the world.**

This quote is associated with Gandhi.

> **We should stop reacting to the world around us and its rapid decay and simply start counteracting this downward spiral by changing one mind at a time by our persistent intent to pursue greater.**

Stop settling for the appetizer by planning and pursuing the main course. The main course is tastier and much more fulfilling. Be a qualitative individual and stop settling for the quantitative ritual of quicker is better. You deserve more than a quickie and a microwave dish. You are the rare cut of beef and that seasonal catch from the sea that can only be found in the best restaurants in the world. Start carrying yourself as how you desire to be treated. If it's not for sale, don't advertise it. If it is for sale don't be cheap in how you package it.

Don't be offended at your initial perception of my words. This can also apply to your work ethic as a professional and your deportment as a lady. If you are single and awaiting God's delivery of your man remember; every man of quality wants to feel as though he is getting the exclusive. He doesn't want what everyone appears to have had.

THE TOTAL PACKAGE

By now, you have certainly tracked the underlining theme of this book as having a holistic approach toward yourselves and the lives God allows to come your way. Use your *Me Time* to empty your cup for the Master's use. If your cup is already empty, then wash out any lingering residue, such as issues from your past that precluded you from service to the Lord. If your cup is clean, then polish out the water spots and cleanser residue and anything else that leaves traces of your fingerprints.

If your cup is residue and fingerprint free, then put it in the right position so that the Master can access it easily without having to search for your willingness. In other words, keep a clean, uncomplicated spirit. Be transparent before God and His people. Be candid when the Lord is in need of you to represent Him.

Above all things, be loving toward His children, whether they are saved or not. Your love and kindness may be the missing ingredients in someone's life when it comes to them being willing to listen to a Christian witness about the Lord.

Perhaps they have heard about the need to give their heart to the Lord but they have never sensed any love from other Christians. God's kingdom won't grow by people transferring from church to church. The Lord's church will grow from new people being won to the Spirit of the One who represents Jesus the best. If I've never seen you laugh, you will never convince me to visit a comedy club. If your hair looks like a bird's nest, you will never convince another woman to try your hair stylist.

You must embody the total package of what you are selling. The only way to represent the total package is when you react instinctively in the way that you have been living privately. Then and only then will the world around you buy what you are selling. This level of consciousness pleases God and will prepare you to live exceedingly and abundantly above your past thought life. Your thought life will eventually dictate your lifestyle and the people and circumstances your life attracts.

CHAPTER SIX
PRICELESS

IT'S A LOT EASIER TO PRACTICE YOUR MISTAKES AS WELL AS YOU R ACCEPTANCE SPEECH IN FRONT OF ONE PERSON. THE GREAT THING ABOUT OUR GOD IS THAT HE SEES US AS THE WINNER IN EITHER CASE.

EXCEEDINGLY AND ABUNDANTLY

By this time of your restoration process, you will find that thoughts and words of encouragement are flowing through you much easier than ever. You have come to the point that you realize that within you resides a true sanctuary. In your previous existence, you rehearsed and harbored thoughts of hatred, rage and resentment. Now you can no longer tolerate their stench. There are no more funeral dirges playing in the back of your mind, beckoning your demise from an overdose of arguments with someone who no longer controls you.

You will discover that you are naturally finding time and taking pleasure in noticing the natural beauty of everything around you. On your morning commute, you may notice the perfect smile and white teeth of a model in a car insurance ad posted on a billboard. The elderly people who once moved through your day as obstacles slow your pace to the point that you stop and notice the graceful way they carry their experience. Your newly garnered wisdom illuminates the notion that if you are blessed to live as long, you too one day will carry yourself with the same pace and care.

Your spirit becomes so in tune with God that you are willing and able to listen instead of doing all the talking. You have grown to t h e point that you w ant to exceedingly, abundantly live for God and bless the people He sends your way. When you achieve such growth, you will instinctively pause the moment your eyes open and say your morning greeting to the Holy Spirit.

You will speak with the same ease and familiarity as you would recite your address because you dwell in this state of mind. You enter your days not seeking personal satisfaction but opportunities to bless your fellow man and brothers and sisters in the faith.

When most hear the phrase "exceedingly and abundantly" it reflects the closing remarks of the prayer from the Apostle Paul to the Ephesians. Paul asserts that they can take comfort in the fact that God is able to do above and beyond all that they can think or comprehend. God's infinite abilities are just one small aspect of His being. When we allow ourselves to become enamored with how big God is we will reach the point of learning to accept what He allows.

You are now ready to pursue ways to please God with the same passion that you previously used to pursue self-satisfaction. It's almost as if you have transformed and become conditioned to act as an arch-enemy of the enemy of God's love. In posing this kind of opposition to Satan, you are willing to sacrifice your thoughts and feelings for pleasing God.

Your life is sold out to the Master, our Lord and Savior, Jesus Christ. This is not the cruel taskmaster that judgmental or plastic Christians push but the One who died for you and transformed your bruises into gemstones. With your outlook changed, you don't perform acts of kindness for the thanks you will receive. You do it for the glory God gets, which never leaves you feeling empty. Now that you have this increased level of spiritual awareness and purpose, I have prepared some life-changing suggestions that you may find fulfilling:

1. Seek and destroy.

This isn't nearly as menacing as it sounds, except for God's enemy. In these missions, your objective is to destroy the frowns and heavy spirits others carry. Strive to put hope in their hearts and a smile on their faces. As idealistic as this sounds, you can accomplish this without putting on a wig with pony tails and bobby socks and skipping around like Pippi Long stocking.

This state of mind is not to be confused with "Random Acts of Kindness." You gear this initiative toward the *spoken* word. Imagine standing at the controls of an arcade video game where you are to aim kind words toward every upside-down frown or grief - stricken spirit who crosses your screen. It looks like this: While standing at a check-out line at a supermarket, you see someone who looks miserable, such as the cashier. Pick out something you admire about that person and compliment them. If it's a female, perhaps her manicure, hair style, accessories or her skin.

Seek and destroy missions aren't for a timid or sensitive personality type. For some, being so personal with a stranger is an absolute no-no. American culture protects the 18 inches of personal space and from becoming too personal with someone. However, the idea here is that most people are dissatisfied in the daily roles they must perform to pay their bills.

Unless the person is confident or the store truly supports their staff, being a cashier is a pretty thankless job. Removing their attention from their task and putting it back on what distinguishes them from that task will make them feel special.

We tend to confuse our purpose with what we do on a day-to-day basis. With a smile, you can put someone in a spirit to greet the next person they meet with a smile. Bear in mind that that next person may be having a rough time and now he or she will encounter a cashier in a better mood. Why? Because your kind words can remind a cashier she is not defined by her task but a person who is destined to change lives. They may act on that by what they see in the person standing behind you in line. Do you see how easy it is to change someone's destiny?

When this happens, the person standing behind you in line—who doesn't even know your name—may leave the store in a better frame of mind for the rest of their day. Had you not been obedient to an opportunity to bless someone, that person may have left even more consumed with their problem, especially after paying for their goods. They may choose to start texting someone as a means to cheer them up. This "pay it forward" chain reaction can change multiple lives.

Do you see the impact you can have just by seeking to offer small kindnesses in God's exceedingly abundant measure? How wonderful will your life become as a repeated result of your desire to seek and destroy sadness? Obviously random acts of kindness work the same way, except in these cases you don't have to utter a word.

You can simply place a five-dollar bill in someone's hand or slow down your pace at the cash register and allow someone else to go first. The down side of pursuing a seek and destroy mission is that someone may reject your words. The other person may even appear offended. Let's face it: the human species is an odd bunch.

Rest assured that if godly reasons motivate you, Jesus is pleased and that is all that matters. Leave the other person to the Holy Spirit and He will tenderize their heart to receive next time. Make sure that if you are rejected, you don't become discouraged, pull into a shell and become cold. The best thing to do is to find another person and be twice as kind. This shows our old sin nature and the enemy of God's love that he didn't win and that you have grown beyond petty thinking. Remember your new level of Christ-like consciousness says that your life and actions are no longer your own. You are now an opponent of the forces of evil that tried to take you out.

2. Keep your hands busy.

You may have heard the cliché: "Idle hands are the devil's workshop." Here is a way to change your brief text messages and e-mail jots to life-changing missives. As our world becomes more adept in the area of social media, why not take a moment to prepare a list of people you haven't spoken to in a while? Better yet, how about a list of the people no-body reaches out to?

In either case, another person will be warmed by the idea that you took the time to remember them enough to share a kind thought. These words don't have to be lengthy and profound, just sincere. You may be surprised at how natural these thoughts become. The fact is you already felt this way.

You are just stirring up the kindness and love you allowed to settle to the bottom of your soulful pot because of life's distractions. If you are a cook you know that the good stuff settles to the bottom of the stew.

Here are some examples of some personal texts, notes and e-mails that I have sent:

- "Hey, just thinking about you. I know it's been a while since we last spoke, but please know that although I'm not talented enough to stay in touch with all the important people in my life, I am loving enough to think about and pray for them regularly. Please know that you're one of those people."

- "Hey, gorgeous. The sun is dimming, so smile."

- "Hey, handsome, how's that Hollywood A-list treating you?"

- "Hey dude I miss you, call a brotha."
- "Remember those long phone calls we used to have? I'm a better person because of them."

- "Sorry to hear that we lost ..., just know they didn't lose their battle, they won the war. They are in the presence of the Lord waiting for the rest of us to come home, so the party can start."

Another great way to uplift people is by simply being an encourager. Encouragers always seek ways to say something complimentary or supportive to people, whether it is needed or not. An encourager always seeks to be a giver rather than a taker. An encourager looks to promote the positive slant of a situation or a person. During times of crisis, an encourager seeks to find the common ground and place the handles to lift everyone up instead of leaving the heavy work for one person.

If an impasse develops during a business meeting or negotiation, then he or she will keep animosity to a minimum and always offer a positive perspective instead of a negative one. When an encourager enters the room he or she becomes the thermostat, changing the room's mood and atmosphere. We all know such people and have been encouraged and guided by their wisdom at pivotal times.

A great practice of an encourager is to ask without prying and offer another, positive perspective even when one isn't solicited. Here is an example. Let's say you were included in an email that contained bad news about someone. You could reply, "We all know what this pain or loss must feel like and if given similar circumstances we would be there too.

Let's remember to lift up our brother or sister in prayer and focus on the many things about them that we love." As ambiguous as this may sound, you get the message.

Taking the courage to be the first or most sincere will bring out the same in others. I'm sure you've seen this happen before. No matter the occasion, just know that as long as your words are sincere they will be timely. People can be pretty complicated and even downright ungrateful at times. Don't do anything kind expecting thanks. All that matters is that you are truly doing this as onto the Lord, the Audience of One.

3. The gift of touch.

This is probably the most significant of initiatives one can pursue relative to human engagement. There are numerous published studies related to the significance of the human touch. You can access some at the National Institute on Mental Health, a federal agency, at www.nimh.nih.org. There are additional studies on the American Psychological Association's website at www.apa.org. In either website, type in the key words, "the results of human touch."

Most studies speak of similar results that touch has on the healing process. Affection and touch have proven to b ring about favorable outcomes in si tuations of stress, autism, depression and anxiety.

There are more than 70 million Americans who suffer from one form or another of mental health illness. Before going any further, we should acknowledge that all of us at one time or another have suffered from some kind of a mental health issue. Most of these issues make us no more deficient as people than suffering from the flu.

Mental illness can be as benign as feeling anxious before your annual job evaluation or as painful as post-traumatic stress disorder. In either case or the dozens in between, the gift of touch goes a long way toward healing. Most people, especially those who live alone, don't often encounter affection regularly. You can make the difference in someone's life by choosing to employ the method of touch. This doesn't mean that you have to go around hugging everyone you encounter (in some instances you may get arrested for harassment).

Having and sharing the gift of touch is all about timing and appropriateness. Standing and sharing a warm conversation with a senior who lives alone is as simple as placing a hand on their shoulder as you speak to punctuate a point or offer the assurance that you care. Giving a hug as you greet someone or as you part company is appropriate and acceptable. If you are sitting across from someone and feel comfortable in touching his or her hand or arm as you speak, you can show warmth and sincerity.

The other person will sense your sincerity as long as you are comfortable. The moment physical touch becomes mechanical or rehearsed it loses its value. If you are a regular part of a religious assembly by way of a synagogue, temple, mosque or church, then hugs, kisses and hearty handshakes are acceptable—maybe even expected. There are many in the se divine meeting places that don't experience affection at any other time in their life, even if they live in a house filled with people.

Remember, sometimes we will be the closest thing to Jesus or a Bible that other people will ever see. At the end of the day, is the Father pleased with the way we are treating each other in the situations He allows to come our way? I know that most of us who are not accustomed to initiating touch may feel awkward. So, in the same way we practice that smooth comeback line in the mirror, we can practice sincerity in our expression of touch.

One of the wonderful things about Jesus is that He could touch someone's soul by just gazing into their eyes. Think about it for a moment. Imagine that the Creator of the universe was walking next to you as He did in the person of Jesus Christ and how awesome it must have felt to look deeply into His eyes. Can you imagine the sense of peace and assurance He conveyed? Now imagine how good we would make Him feel if we prayed for the same ability to grasp each other's soul and encourage one another with just one touch. That is possible.

THE CHRISTMAS CHALLENGE

Funny place to find the word, *Christmas,* huh? You might expect to hear about the option of the Christmas spirit at that time of year when we are in a good mood almost every day. I took this prompt from my weekly e-mail devotional called *Snack Food for the Soul,* which has a worldwide readership of about 14,000 people. It is a short read I send out every Monday morning at midnight. Its premise is to capture your mind's ability to soar outside of every-day thought processes, and make you think about how God sees things. (If you are interested in receiving these you may log onto www.freedomperspectiveministries.com and sign up. I promise you won't be disappointed).

During the week of Christmas in 2010 I wrote a devotional for my Snack Food family called "The Christmas Challenge." Its theme is to encourage people to personally keep the Christmas cheer by becoming the Christmas cheer every day. Many believers complain about the commercialization of Christmas and gift giving, yet they don't focus enough on giving Christ His gifts through the ways we treat each other daily. After all, it is His birthday, shouldn't we give Him something? Here is the devotional:

The world over, Christmas is the happiest time

of the year. Even the most stone-faced and hard-hearted individuals soften and reveal the child that drives each and every one of us. It is within this season that we all arrive on common ground and agree to be the most Christ-like that we have collectively been all year.

We don't know why, but there is an air of expectation and joyous laughter, either on our faces or in our hearts. We all take turns doing good deeds as though we believe it is the right thing to do. We take survey of our blessings and good fortune and see within our means whom we can bless and whom we can cheer up.

Those who are saddened and broken-hearted with hurts and the memories of those who have passed on receive unexpected expressions of Christ's love. Ahhh, Christmas, the season that brings new cheer, joy and merriment that seems lost throughout the year. This season called Christmas, which celebrates the Christ of all who live far and near. Christmas, oh sweet Christmas, your intent is very clear: that our risen Savior will live in the daily lives we hold so dear. Holy Spirit, our Guide and Counselor left to us by our risen Savior, take us by our soul's hand and lead us through the path that our Savior trod.

Remind us that in spite of how we would one day be, He still decided it was there He should suffer. He miserably bled, but not to just die. He rose again to guarantee that the enemy's soul of our lives will one day be eternally dead.

As we consider our family and vacation plans the next two weeks, let's remember that the wise men brought Him gifts in honor of His majesty and His promise. We will give love and valued things to our loved ones—deservedly so—but let's not forget to give something to the Lord who we have asked so much from this past year.

So, what do you give the King of all creation that can fathom the metrics of millions of galaxies? You give Him back what He brought you here for. According to Luke 10:27, Jesus said, *"'Love the Lord your God with all your heart and with all your soul and with all your strength and with all your mind'; and, 'Love your neighbor as yourself.'"*

Jesus doesn't want your Bentley, American Express Black Card, or a ride in your Gulf Stream V-SP private jet. You may think He is impressed with your volunteer time feeding the homeless or even giving them the spare change collecting with the lint in the bottom of your pocket. You know what He truly wants this Christmas?

The same thing any parent would want to see every day. He wants to see His children get along and treat each other with the same love that we would want shown toward ourselves.

Giving what you have in abundance or what you give on a scheduled day for a pre-determined amount of time is wonderful and should be highly commended by man. But God will only honor it if it is done with the intent of love that you expect from God our Father.

This Christmas, say "Happy Birthday" to Jesus and bring His majesty a gift by:

1. Calling someone who is all alone and lonely and telling him or her they were on your mind.
2. Forgive someone's actions or quirky ways in spite of self-respect or popular opinion. After you have swallowed the bitter taste of your pride, tell the Lord this is for Calvary.
3. Give something more in your tithes, offerings or to another soul. Even if it's more than you're accustomed to, if it's not enough for a need, then it's for a seed.
4. Give up a secret sin or two and ask the Lord to remove the taste and desire from your heart forever, and to replace the void with the joy of knowing that you are available to move that much closer to Him.

5. Decide not to judge anyone anymore, because "'I tell you the truth, whatever you did for one of the least of these brothers of mine, you did for me.'" (Matthew 25:40).

The key words in that last passage are "for me." This Christmas season, please remember this season is for Him. So my beloved brothers and sisters, let us please remember to give Jesus' love to each other so that He may receive it in return. I pray that the complete joy of our Lord and the unwavering peace of His countenance rest heavily upon, around and throughout your life and everything and everyone you love and touch. The Lord's intent for you is my desperate prayer for you. In Jesus name. Amen!!!

Simple isn't it? If we realized how in love the Lord truly is with us, we would not hesitate returning this love to Him through our brothers and sisters.

PLAY WELL WITH OTHERS

Sound familiar? This is o ne of the more difficult internal changes to make. As people, most of us tend to size someone up as soon as they approach us. As soon as we see someone's face, walk or outfit, we determine in our minds if we are going to like or dislike them. Some of us even determine if we are going to like someone by looking at the quality of their shoes. At this point in your life and restoration, be more concerned with how the Lord feels about your thought process.

When you meet someone try to take on an attitude that says, "I get to meet another family member today." If they are not in Christ then look at it as, "I hope my relationship with the Lord is such that they will feel as though my brand of Christianity is one that they want to embrace." Try not to become the girl you once were in grade school.

If the woman you meet looks three times better than you feel about yourself, don't become her worst critic. In fact, you should know by now that the prettiest, apparently most pulled-together women can have the greatest degree of heartache. Some of these good-looking women who seemingly "have it going on" have had nothing but phony people to contend with.

Imagine you have always been the girl who all the guys were after and, because of that, was the object of all the other girls' scorn or affection. The latter meant that you would have people putting their best foot forward just to impress you and win your affections or friendship.

No one would stop to take interest in your fears and innermost thoughts. You would constantly have people in your face, trying to be who they're not; imagine being lied to every day of a friendship.

So the next time you see a striking woman with princess features and flawless body, don't assume she is arrogant or a phony. There are some beautiful, intellectual women who have to dumb down their speech just to be accepted. There are also some high-powered women who are judges, lawyers, doctors, politicians, clergy or businesspersons and just want a friend with whom they can let their hair down.

Let's face it, most guys are too insecure to handle a woman who is brighter than them. Maybe, just maybe, you could be that friend that articulate person has been looking for; remember to love the skin you're in and so will everyone else.

THIS IS FOR CALVARY

No statement of faith declares your commitment for the sake of Christ more than this one: *This is for Calvary.* This is where the rubber meets the road and places a demarcation on your lifeline. It says I am positioning myself for the most incredible supernatural chain of events to occur in your life. *For the sake of Calvary* summons the atmosphere's attention to the fact that something great is about to be done in the earthly realm that will line up with God's will.

When you take this stance, it means your flesh has fallen in line with the Holy Spirit's leading. Your mind and your desire to please self are no longer in control. Take note that this is one of the times in your life when faith becomes the substance of things hoped for and the evidence of things not seen (Hebrews 11:1).

Your intended actions were as sure to you as the fact that the chair you are sitting on would have supported your weight when you sat down.

Here are some examples of those "**Calvary moments**:"

1. You are absolutely terrified of getting up in front of people because you are so shy that you would rather die quietly in a corner than yell out, "I think I'm having a heart attack!" At a major, job-related function, you notice one of the key executives enter the room. You and everyone else are well aware that he is undergoing chemotherapy for an aggressive form of cancer. He is moving slowly and appears a bit disoriented. Everyone is too intimidated to acknowledge this. However, a Calvary moment gives you the grace

to walk over to him, offering a handshake and a warm hug as you tell him that you have been praying for him and are inspired by his courage and tenacious example of leadership.

You may feel that not too many people would feel that this is appropriate or acceptable. The fact is you are right. But think of it this way: this will become a pivotal moment in both your lives, likely more yours than his. He is dealing with needing a far more challenging level of courage than you.

Still, he will be touched that out of this crowd, someone thought enough of him to show kindness. Your life will change forever because you seized the moment like Peter did when Jesus called him to walk on water. The difference is that you didn't begin to sink.

2. A total stranger is about to take the stage at a major outdoor event and you notice her beautiful, flared leg, white flowing summer pants and fabulous, strappy sandals. Yet, as she passes by, you notice a bright red stain in the most embarrassing place. Instantly you know the dread that she will encounter if she walks onstage without noticing.

You quickly remove your shawl, run over to her and discreetly whisper your observation into her ear. She takes the shawl and wraps it around her waist as if nothing occurred. As she continues with her speech, your eyes meet and you see smiling eyes of gratitude. The only approval that is stronger is the inner peace of the Holy Spirit's covering.

3. You are the last to arrive at the table to have lunch with friends. As you sit and greet them, you see someone at another table staring at you with an evil glare. You ignore these piercing eyes and continue enjoying your company. Twenty minutes later you get up to use the ladies room and on your way back to your table, notice you missed a call on your cell phone. As you stop to check your messages you see the glaring woman walking directly toward you, as if she wants to confront you. You finish your call but as soon as you put your phone away she starts yelling and screaming at you like a lunatic.

Then, just as quickly, she walks away. You start to turn toward her to give her a piece of your mind, but the same calm that allowed you to take her verbal tirade dictates that you simply take a deep breath. You look around; only a few employees saw this spectacle.

They look at you as though you are at fault and go back to work. As you get back to your friends, you start to say, "The freakiest thing just happened to me..." However, before you can finish, a much older lady who reminds you of your grandmother gently approaches and says, "My dear, I am so sorry for the behavior of my daughter."

Everybody at your table looks up in disbelief. The lady goes on to explain that her daughter is suffering from dementia and suffers these outbursts for no reason. She adds, "One of the waiters came over to m e and told me what happened. He assumed that my daughter had an illness and thought it best that I know. He told me of your total understanding."

As the woman continues speaking, she bursts into tears and can't stop commending you for being so kind and showing that all humanity is not lost. She asks you if you are a Christian and you say, "Yes. So are my friends." She replies, "I am so glad that all of God's people still continue to show each other His love."

While her comment blesses you, the restraint the Holy Spirit placed within you blesses you even more. You realized that if you reacted in an-all-too-human manner, this incident would not have had a happy ending.

ALL THAT MATTERS

Wondering why these examples had to be so involved and specific? The answer: they are all true stories that real people just like you have experienced. They all had one thing in common. These people's human nature would ordinarily have led them to behave completely the opposite, but they all shared the same encounter with Christ.

In the first scenario, this woman was reading her Bible one night and was taken by the story of Christ's very human moment in the Garden of Gethsemane, when He asked God to relieve Him of having to face what lay ahead of Him. She instantly broke down and fell on her face on her bedroom floor, hysterically crying. She realized that He didn't really want to die, nor did He want to endure public flogging and humiliation. What gripped her soul was the Lord's statement, "Nevertheless not my will but Yours be done." She knew that His love for her had changed His mind.

For the woman in scenario number two, her epiphany came when she was having an adulterous affair that lasted almost three months. Her husband was ill and she started to feel weak in her sexual desires. Although she knew she would never leave him, she still missed being satisfied sexually. One day through a chain of events the enemy allowed temptation to slip in and exploited her vulnerability.

After three months she decided to end her sinful union. He left without making things difficult for her, except for one thing. He told her she should get tested for AIDS, admitting he knew about it all along but didn't care. The horror of what she put herself through while exposing her innocent husband to risk was almost more than she could bear. The test result came back negative; she realized that she had dodged the bullet.

A few weeks later she got a phone call from her aunt, who had dreamt that her niece was having an affair. The aunt said that God covered her in her sin because she cared for her husband for three years without complaining. That word from God caused her to seek ways in which she could serve anyone who is in need. She promised the Lord that she would never allow someone to be exposed the way she had been.

The last scenario was simple to grasp. The young woman on the receiving end of the tongue lashing used to be the type who would act before thinking. Her claim to fame was the ability to use the kind of profanity that might have made Satan blush. Her Damascus Road experience occurred when she suffered a stroke that left her temporarily unable to speak. She told the Lord that if He would give her back her speech that she would never again use her mouth for filth. The rest is history.

What is your Calvary moment? Where in your life did you determine that the part of your character that offended the Lord the most should die for Him the way He died for you?

It's that simple. You have to de cide whether you love Him that much, just as He thought about it in the Garden and looked down through time and saw what was about to happen in your innocent life that would scar you the way it did. He decided that His scars would heal, but if He didn't endure the cross your scars would never heal. Isn't the Lord good? Do you now see how your pain was an appraisal for the redemptive value you feel now?

WHAT NOW?

Now that you and I have gotten to know each other a little better in the spirit, please understand that I have been praying for you throughout every paragraph written on these pages. My desire is that you can go through life without any burdens. You are not the sum total of what you have experienced. You are the sum total of what you see God as today. Yesterday is gone and is never returning. Today is a gift from God, so thank Him by living it the way He told you to in His Word. Tomorrow is not here yet, so don't worry about what it will bring, just concern yourself with the fact that tomorrow belongs to He who measures the universe within the hollow of His hand.

For at least one day a week do as author, William W. Purkey celebrates in his words:

"You've gotta dance like there's nobody watching, Love like you'll never be hurt, Sing like there's nobody listening, And live like it's heaven on earth."
(--From http://www.goodreads.com/quotes/show/10123)

Stop taking yourself and your life so seriously. Lighten up and show the world around you that the joy of the Lord is your strength. The world didn't give you strength, so it certainly can't take it away. Tell the Lord that you are now free from your past so that you can now embrace your future.

Live by His words, *"Let your light shine before men, that they may see your good deeds and praise your Father in heaven."* (Matthew 5:16 KJV).

Father God, in the name of Jesus, I thank you for my beloved sisters, brothers, and friends who have had more time invested in their healing process than I have had in writing these words. Lord, I know that You have seen and heard all that they have suffered through. Now, Lord, I ask that You show them a preview of the coming attractions in life that will come from serving You and realizing the fulfillment that will bring.

Thank you, Lord, for the purpose that is waiting for each reader on the other side of his or her prayer. Holy Spirit, help to eliminate the multiple choices in their lives so that they can focus on the path ahead without the distraction of the past or those who don't want them to progress. Holy

Spirit, keep them in the center of your will. Father, continue to inspire and encourage each person reading these words to seek You and You alone, the Audience of O ne. In Jesus, mighty name. Amen!!!

Log onto www.trueperspectivepublishing.com to keep up with other book titles in The Power of Perspective book series. Future titles will include children's books targeted at self and spiritual-awareness and character development. Future titles will also deal with more specific subject and matter dealt with in The Power of Perspective part one.

You may also subscribe to receive by email Snack Food for the Soul, our weekly brief life-enhancing devotional that has literally changed thousands of lives through-out the world. If you are an aspiring author, the True Perspective Publishing House may be the instrument to help you tell your story by eliminating the intimidation from the publishing process.

Log on to www.trueperspectivepublishing.com to find out more about leaving your literary mark in this life.

SEAN CORT

Sean's multi-industry repertoire spans 25 years as an award winning veteran hosting, writing, producing and marketing for every medium in communications today. Sean is President and Founder of The Healing Continuum.com, a health based initiative designed to increase health literacy for women and the lives they touch.

As a highly proclaimed "Perspective Coach" and ordained Elder. Sean has addressed stadium audiences of 75,000 people. Sean's book, ***The Power of Perspective*** and the marketing genius of his Power of Perspective brand empowers individuals to see life's circumstances and how they interconnect us from multiple perspectives upon demand. This holistic view of life teaches people how to se e the results of their actions before they react. This perspective now competently puts us in the driver's seat toward our destiny.

Sean Blogs for Psychology Today.com and is a Mental Health Examiner for The Orlando Examiner. He serves on several academic and non-profit boards and consults various aspects of private and public industry where he is a vital part of their thought and planning process. Sean's gifting is in identifying the detail in complexity and making it plain for the individual to understand while motivating the masses toward a common goal through empathy and assimilation.

Sean's passion for writing and communicating drove him to launch the True Perspective Publishing House; where he is be able to showcase His ministry of changing mankind's thought process toward a more Godly Perspective. The True Perspective Publishing mission is *"to thoroughly empower each of our authors with proficiency and access to tell their story without boundaries.*

Sean's Vision Statement as a Speaker, Perspective Coach and Publisher is *"There is a chord of commonality that is interwoven within every being within the human family. Although ideologies and geographical locale may separate us; it is the hope of True Perspective Publishing that our books and authors may identify that chord, which is the Spirit of God more readily to the eye and heart of mankind.*

Sean also authors **Snack Food for the Soul**, a weekly newsletter that inspires and challenges the thought process of its thousands of readers worldwide. Sean's extended bio can be found on his website
www.freedomperspectiveministries.com

NOTES:

NOTES:

www.ingramcontent.com/pod-product-compliance
Lightning Source LLC
Chambersburg PA
CBHW030929090426
42737CB00007B/369